# Navigating the News

# Navigating the News

## A Political Media User's Guide

Michael Baranowski

 PRAEGER

AN IMPRINT OF ABC-CLIO, LLC
Santa Barbara, California • Denver, Colorado • Oxford, England

Copyright 2013 by Michael Baranowski

All rights reserved. No part of this publication may be reproduced, stored in a retrieval system, or transmitted, in any form or by any means, electronic, mechanical, photocopying, recording, or otherwise, except for the inclusion of brief quotations in a review, without prior permission in writing from the publisher.

**Library of Congress Cataloging-in-Publication Data**

Baranowski, Michael.
    Navigating the news : a political media user's guide / Michael Baranowski.
        p. cm.
    Includes bibliographical references and index.
        ISBN 978–1–4408–0321–5 (hardback) — ISBN 978–1–4408–0322–2 (ebook) 1. Mass media—Political aspects—United States. 2. Press and politics—United States. 3. Communication in politics—United States. 4. Communication in politics—United States—Public opinion. 5. Mass media—Political aspects—United States—Public opinion. 6. United States—Politics and government. I. Title.
P95.82.U6B37 2013
070.4′493240973—dc23          2013007799

ISBN: 978–1–4408–0321–5
EISBN: 978–1–4408–0322–2

17  16  15  14  13      1  2  3  4  5

This book is also available on the World Wide Web as an eBook.
Visit www.abc-clio.com for details.

Praeger
An Imprint of ABC-CLIO, LLC

ABC-CLIO, LLC
130 Cremona Drive, P.O. Box 1911
Santa Barbara, California 93116-1911

This book is printed on acid-free paper ∞

Manufactured in the United States of America

*For Mom and Dad*

# Contents

# Acknowledgments

First and foremost, I'd like to thank William Norman, who carefully reviewed several drafts of this book and responded with copious notes. He took all my importuning in stride and provided tons of helpful suggestions as well as the occasional grammar tip (while I still don't think punctuation should go inside quotation marks, I've given up that fight thanks to his repeated, yet always tactful, reminders). I can't imagine having done this without him. Thanks also to Billie Jo Wood and Jennifer Taylor, two extraordinary students and great readers who commented on drafts of the book. My mother, Barbara Baranowski, also read an earlier draft and used her grammatical expertise, honed by decades as a junior high English teacher, to point out things I might have caught had I only paid more attention to her when I was growing up. Steve Catalano, my editor at Praeger, has been great to work with, and I truly appreciate his arranging for a much-needed extension when I ran into a rough patch. Finally, thanks to my wife Kimberly for her sympathetic ear, emotional support, and for being my most favorite person.

# ONE

## Introduction to the News

October 4, 2012, was a really big day for the news media. It was the day after the first presidential debate, in which President Obama had been absolutely obliterated by Mitt Romney. Up to that point, Obama had been slowly but steadily pulling away from Romney—on the day of the debate, polling showed Obama with a comfortable lead, on pace to pick up 332 electoral votes, well over the 270 needed to win the presidency.[1] But according to the media, the debate suddenly changed *everything*. *Time*'s Joel Klein called it "one of the most inept performances I've ever seen by a sitting President."[2] Andrew Sullivan, writing for the *Daily Beast* website, captured the sense of near-panic among Obama partisans with an article titled "Did Obama Just Throw the Entire Election Away?"[3] In less than a day, the media narrative of the 2012 campaign had shifted so much in favor of Romney that *National Journal* felt the need to run an article on "5 Reasons Why It's Too Early to Write Off Obama."[4]

It turned out that it *was* too early to write off President Obama, who ended up winning a race that wasn't nearly as close as many in the media predicted. Far from being a toss-up, the election went decisively for Obama, who finished with 332 electoral votes—exactly the number projected on the day of the debate that supposedly "changed everything."

You might be inclined to write this off as an isolated incident—except it wasn't. For years, political scientists have been saying that debates don't really matter much in presidential elections. And they have plenty of hard data to prove it. Debates often give candidates a bump in support, say the experts, but that boost in popularity almost always fades over time. In fact, even the campaigns themselves aren't necessarily all that important. Political scientist Allan Lictman, who has been studying presidential elections for over 30 years, believes that presidential elections are like earthquakes—driven by deep forces over which even the best campaigns have very little control. Since he developed his theory in the early 1980s, Lictman has correctly predicted the popular vote winner in every presidential election, naming the eventual winner long before Election Day. Lictman called the 2012 election for Obama way back in January—January of *2010*, nearly a year and a half before President Obama even had a Republican opponent. When asked what this tells us about media coverage of elections, Lictman said, "It means it's all about the wrong things. Primarily, elections are responsive to these much deeper forces. Focusing on the campaign is like focusing on the froth of the wave, instead of the wave itself."[5]

Yet election after election, the media keep on focusing on the froth. While it's possible to find serious, substantive political coverage in the media, if you don't know where and how to look, chances are you'll end up with a highly superficial and deeply misleading view of politics—a whole lot of froth, amounting to very little.

## MEDIA MATTERS

No matter who you are or how closely you follow politics, you get just about all of your political information from the media. For nearly everyone, being well informed about politics requires spending some time with political media. These days, it may be more important than ever to be well informed about politics—but not because "Obama wants to destroy the country," or "Republicans hate minorities," or whatever other horror people think is being inflicted on the country by the evil, insane, or congenitally stupid opposition. Being well informed is important because more people can participate in politics, and politicians are paying closer attention to the public than ever before. In other words, politics has become a lot more democratic.* This is partly due to more people being legally allowed to vote, thanks to federal legislation (the Voting Rights Act of 1965 in particular), as well as the 26th Amendment (ratified in 1971) that lowered the national voting age to 18. The importance of the public may be even greater in primary elections, where the Democrats and Republicans choose their party's

---

*That's "small-d" democratic, meaning more people-centered, as opposed to "big-D" Democratic, which refers to the Democratic Party. Some Republicans refer to the Democratic Party as the "Democrat Party" to make the distinction more clear.

nominees for office. While people have been voting in primaries for a long time, up until the 1970s party leaders could, and sometimes did, reject the choice of the voters. That's something that doesn't happen anymore.*

Technology has also played an important role in the democratization of politics. Politicians have always cared about public opinion, but it wasn't until the 1950s that they could hope to measure it in any regular and systematic way. And it was another 30 years before computers became powerful and inexpensive enough to make public opinion polling not just commonplace but an absolute necessity for any candidate for high political office. A twenty-first-century politician who doesn't bother to regularly check in with public opinion isn't likely to hold office for very long.

You may think that it's easier than ever to be well informed about politics, what with 24/7 political coverage on TV, the Internet, talk radio, and even old-fashioned print media. There's no question that we have more choices than ever when it comes to political news and information, but many of these choices aren't so good. In fact, many of these choices can actually make things worse by leaving people with the impression that they understand much more about politics than they really do. Uninformed citizens are bad enough, but uninformed citizens who *think* they're informed are even worse. Unfortunately, immersion in political news is no guarantee of understanding. As we'll see, people who devote immense amounts of time to political news can actually be more misinformed and less reasonable than those of us who spend far less time following politics. Having a lot of information is no protection against being wrong: it's the quality of the information, as well as our ability to interpret it in a rational and unbiased fashion, that's really important.

Even if the United States is filled with politically clueless people, it may not be such a big deal if they balance each other out. In this view, mass political opinion can be sort of like guessing the number of marbles in a pickle jar. Most people's guesses will miss the mark, but the average guess of a large enough crowd is generally very accurate. The idea that the masses generally come up with good overall decisions is sometimes referred to as the "wisdom of crowds," and it really does work amazingly well for some things. The problem is that in politics we don't see the pickle jar for ourselves—we view it through the lens of the media, and the media show us a distorted view of politics. This goes a lot further than liberal or conservative bias. (In fact, ideological distortion may be one of the less important types of bias in the media.) Even if we could somehow get a clear view of the political pickle jar, it turns out that we're biased too, meaning that we bring our

---

*Much to the dismay of many Republican and Democratic elites.

own distortions to the political news we get. The bad news is that there's no way to permanently "fix" these biases. The good news is that if we are at least aware of them—both in the media and in ourselves—we can minimize the likelihood that they'll throw off our political judgment.

## WHAT IS THE NEWS?

If you're going to successfully navigate the news, you need to start by understanding what news actually is. This may seem odd because you've probably never considered the meaning of news. It's just—well, *news*, stuff that happens. You know it when you see it. But we can often learn a lot about something when we take a close look at its meaning— especially when it's something we're not used to thinking much about.

To start with, we can break news into a few really broad categories: political news, business news, entertainment news, and so on. Our focus is on political news, which you might be tempted to define as "news about politics." That's absolutely true, but as a definition it's also absolutely use-less because it doesn't tell us anything. In attempting to come up with a non-useless definition of political news, we quickly run into the "What do you mean by 'political'?" problem. In other words, we can't expect to come up with a useful definition of political news until we're reasonably clear on what politics is. One popular definition of politics in political science circles is "the study of who gets what, when, and how." The problem with this definition is that it encompasses just about everything, from presidential elections to a Cub Scout meeting. The politics we'll be looking at in this book is far narrower, focusing solely on governmental affairs, but it has the considerable advantage of limiting our focus so that we're not considering, for instance, the politics of Harry Potter.*

## NEWS VERSUS "THE NEWS"

As long as there have been governments, there has been political news. Long before the Internet, TV, or even movable type, people were talking, griping, and pontificating about what government was (or wasn't) doing. But because government does so much and involves so many people, there's no way anyone can possibly digest all of the raw data about it. In order to have anything approaching a useful view of government, we need political news to be edited and summarized for us.

---

*This is not a made-up thing. "Politics of Harry Potter" even has its very own Wikipedia entry.

The result of this process is The News. The News is information about politics as it is produced, packaged, and presented through media. The News is, in other words, a *product* that someone is looking to make a buck on.* Literally everyone who follows politics gets most, and in many cases all, of their information from The News. This is really important because, for reasons we'll be looking at throughout the book, The News systematically distorts our view of politics. In the end, The News is whatever media companies think we'll consume. And for the most part, it turns out that what we ask for—and what we end up getting—as consumers isn't all that good for us as citizens.

The media is sometimes referred to as the fourth branch of government because of its critical role in informing the people. If you measure "informing the people" in terms of the amount of The News that's being produced, then this is unquestionably the Golden Age of media. Until not all that long ago, most people had a very limited number of choices for political news. There was a daily local paper, whatever nightly news show you might watch (with a grand total of three options), and maybe the weekly edition of *Time* or *Newsweek*. Real political junkies might supplement this meager menu with a subscription to the *New York Times*, *Wall Street Journal*, or *Washington Post*, assuming they could even get daily delivery where they lived.

That world is long gone, and we generally see our vastly expanded news choices as a good thing. But attempting to find some coherence in this modern torrent of political information can feel like trying to drink out of a fire hose. It's understandable that many people simply throw up their hands in frustration. But with a little bit of guidance, you can better direct and control the intimidatingly powerful flow of The News and emerge a more informed citizen.

## WHERE PEOPLE GET THEIR NEWS

While there are a staggering number of political news sources, nearly all of them can be grouped into one of three basic categories. The first, and oldest, is print, which consists of news that you read anywhere except on a screen. Essentially, this means newspapers and magazines. Books don't count because people don't get The News from books. That's not at all to say that books aren't an important source of political understanding because they most definitely are. But despite their great value, books can't provide news because by the time a book can be written, edited, and published, any

---

*There are millions of unpaid people who blog, post, and tweet about politics every single day. But just like the rest of us, they're almost entirely dependent on The News for their raw material.

news in it is no longer current (which means it's no longer news). Next is broadcast news, which consists of television and radio. Finally, there's online media, which is any news that you get from the Internet. Not all of these sources are equally popular, as you can see in Figure 1.1.

You can see some pretty clear trends in this chart, one of which is the rapid rise of the Internet as a news source, as well as the not-coincidental decline of newspapers. This is to be expected because before the Internet newspapers had a virtual monopoly on news in print. Magazines have never been much of a factor because newspapers, with their far-more-frequent publication schedule, get the news out much faster. (And in the same way newspapers are able to beat out magazines, we now see online news beating out newspapers.)

Another important thing to notice is that while the Internet is what captures the most attention, TV news is still clearly dominant. Most people are surprised by this, which tells us a lot about how The News works. There's nothing novel about a story on how TV is still the most popular news source. It's a lot more interesting to talk about the Internet, social media, smartphones, and iPad apps. In the process, though, we end up with a distorted view of reality.

## HOW POPULAR IS THE NEWS?

The most popular news programs on TV are the half-hour national network news shows presented by ABC, CBS, and NBC. In 2011, the top-rated NBC *Nightly News* averaged 8.75 million viewers, with ABC's

**Figure 1.1.   Where Americans Get Their News**

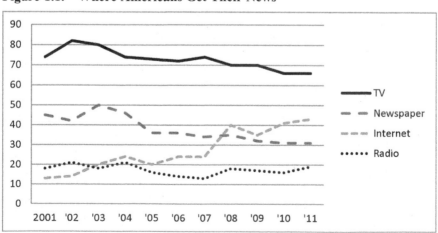

*World News* at 7.82 million viewers and CBS's *Evening News* at 5.97 million trailing the pack.[6] The most popular cable TV politics show, Fox's *The O'Reilly Factor*, pulled in just under 3 million viewers a night. Stretching the definition of news a bit more, Comedy Central's *The Daily Show with Jon Stewart* and *The Colbert Report* each get around million viewers, with Stewart drawing a slightly larger audience than Colbert.[7] By way of comparison, the most watched regularly broadcast show of 2011—*NBC Sunday Night Football*—averaged just over 20 million viewers per week, with the most popular nonsporting-event shows of that year, *American Idol* and *NCIS*, averaging slightly under 20 million viewers.[8]

The network news numbers are a lot better than any newspaper can claim. Of the national newspapers, the *Wall Street Journal* leads the pack with a circulation of 2.3 million, followed closely by *USA Today* at about 1.7 million and the *New York Times* at 1.6 million.[9] It would be nice if we could also include news websites in this, but we can't because nobody has come up with a way of making a really usable comparison between newspaper circulation and website viewing. The most commonly used measure—the pageview—only tells us how many people end up on a webpage of a site. To make a fair comparison between pageviews and newspaper circulation, we'd need to know how many stories from the daily newspaper people looked at, which is next to impossible.

## THE MEDIUM MATTERS

One of the most important books ever written about the influence of television is Neil Postman's *Amusing Ourselves to Death*. The central point Postman makes in his book is that television is different from any medium that came before it, and that this difference matters a lot. He concludes that "[Most people] have difficulty accepting the truth, if they think about it at all, that not all forms of discourse can be converted from one medium to another. It is naïve to suppose that something that has been expressed in one form can be expressed in another without significantly changing its meaning, texture or value."[10]

If you think about where you get your political information, you probably think in terms of the source, which you may readily admit makes a difference. For instance, many people realize that Fox News reports many of the same political stories differently than the CBS *Evening News*, and that the *New York Times* and the *Wall Street Journal* often have clearly different takes on the same political event.

What Postman is talking about, though, goes much deeper than this. He's saying that the medium—in other words, the *transmission device*—for the story affects how it's told. In this view, a news story reported on a Fox News TV segment is a very different thing from the same news story reported on the Fox News website. This is a much deeper, and far less common, way of thinking about the news. To understand how this can be possible and why it matters so much, we'll need to take a closer look at the basic types of media, which we do in Chapter 2.

## NOTES

1. "ElectoralVote," accessed November 10, 2012. http://www.electoralvote.com/evp2012/Pres/Maps/Oct03.html.

2. Joe Klein, "Obama's Debate Strategy: Unilateral Disarmament?" *Time*, http://swampland.time.com/2012/10/03/the-debate/.

3. Andrew Sullivan, "Did Obama Just Throw the Entire Election Away?" *Andrew Sullivan—The Dish*, October 8, 2012, http://andrewsullivan.thedailybeast.com/2012/10/did-obama-just-throw-the-entire-election-away.html (accessed December 18. 2012).

4. Ron Fournier, "5 Reasons Why It's Too Early to Write Off Obama," *NationalJournal.com*, October 4, 2012, http://www.nationaljournal.com/2012-presidential-campaign/5-reasons-why-it-s-too-early-to-write-off-obama-20121004.

5. Shankar Vedantam, "What Earthquakes Can Teach Us about Elections," NPR.org, November 9, 2012, http://m.npr.org/news/front/164711093.

6. "Network: By the Numbers," Pew Research Center, accessed December 21, 2012, http://stateofthemedia.org/2012/network-news-the-pace-of-change-accelerates/network-by-the-numbers/.

7. *O'Reilly Factor* ratings from "Cable: By the Numbers," Pew Research Center, accessed December 21, 2012, http://stateofthemedia.org/2012/cable-cnn-ends-its-ratings-slide-fox-falls-again/cable-by-the-numbers/. *Daily Show* and *Colbert Report* ratings from "2011 Ratings Release," Comedy Central, accessed December 21, 2012, http://www.comedycentral.com/press/press_releases/2011/122011-2011-ratings-release.jhtml.

8. Lisa de Moraes, "What Were the Top 10 Most-watched Shows This Season?" *The Washington Post—Blogs*, May 24, 2012, http://www.washingtonpost.com/blogs/tv-column/post/what-were-the-top-10-most-watched-shows-this-season/2012/05/23/gJQANudXlU_blog.html.

9. Circulation numbers from the Alliance for Audited Media September 20, 2012 report, http://abcas3.auditedmedia.com/ecirc/newstitlesearchus.asp.

10. Neil Postman, *Amusing Ourselves to Death: Public Discourse in the Age of Show Business*, 20th Anniversary Edition (New York: Penguin, 2005), 117.

# TWO

## Types of Media

### OLD SCHOOL NEWS: PRINT MEDIA

Political news has been in print for a really long time. One of the first print news publishers was Julius Caesar, who established a daily record of Roman government activities called the *Acta Diurna*. While it didn't feature hard-hitting investigative reporting or in-depth analysis of the latest war with the Gauls, the *Acta Diurna* gave Roman citizens basic information about what their government was up to, something that hadn't been available up to that time. (Naturally, all stories were subject to Caesar's approval) But you couldn't get home delivery or pick up a copy at the market because the *Acta Diurna* wasn't a newspaper—its news was chiseled into stone tablets that were then posted in public spaces, making it more of a bulletin board (a really heavy bulletin board) than a newspaper.

This approach to news was more than a little inconvenient, but it was pretty much state of the art given the technology available in those days. Movable type wouldn't be invented for over a thousand years, and it would take 500 more years until that Chinese innovation made its way to Europe. Movable type was a big deal because it allowed publishers to turn out multiple copies of printed materials far more quickly, accurately, and inexpensively than anything that had come before. Even so, printing was still far too slow and expensive to make it possible to regularly produce a large-circulation newspaper.

The first true newspapers wouldn't appear until the early 1600s, and almost a century more passed before the emergence of successful daily papers. These newspapers were skimpy little things that had nothing like the mass circulation of modern metropolitan dailies. The political content of these early papers would seem incredibly biased to us, which is exactly what their publishers intended. Newspapers were often designed to be tools of political parties, who used the papers to keep in contact with their voters. This made good business sense for the papers because it gave them a reliable subscriber base from among the party faithful.

The first modern U.S. newspaper was the *New York Sun*, which began publication in 1833. Two years later, it was followed by another New York paper, the *Herald*. The *Sun* and *Herald* were the first major "penny papers" which, as you probably guessed, sold for the unheard-of price of a single penny. Previously, newspapers had been commonly selling for six cents a copy, making the *Sun* and *Herald* big bargains.* What allowed them to lower their cost was an important technological advance—the steam-powered printing press. Prior to this, presses were operated by hand and could only crank out somewhere between several hundred to a thousand pages per hour. The new technology quickly doubled and then quadrupled this speed, making it easier and cheaper for publishers to print. The result was affordable daily news for the general public.

The next new technology to transform print media was the telegraph, which made it possible for newspapers to provide next-day coverage of events from coast to coast. Although the telegraph was invented at around the same time as the steam-powered press, it wasn't until the mid-1840s that it became commonplace, mainly because it took a while to string all those telegraph lines. The ability to give people truly current news from anywhere (at least anywhere connected by telegraph lines) quickly led to the development of "wire services" like the Associated Press, which used the telegraph to compile and distribute news to papers all across the country.

Now that newspapers could report current news from anywhere and profitably sell it to a mass audience, the industry took off. This also affected *how* the news was reported. Publishers began to realize that they could attract larger audiences with national news, but that doing so meant abandoning their close political party ties—ties that would alienate a large percentage of potential readers. "Objective" news suddenly made good economic sense, a fact far more important to the spread of nonpartisan journalism than any lofty ideas about reporting "the truth" for its own sake.

---

*Five cents may seem like nothing to you, but people earned a lot less back then. In today's terms, it was like charging a quarter when the competition was asking $1.25.

As Alex Jones, director of Harvard's Shorenstein Center in the Press and Public Policy, puts it, "objectivity was a commercial necessity that was turned into a virtue by its advocates, who saw news without political bias as a desirable side effect of what was essentially a matter of self-interest."[1]

Newspaper audiences continued to grow throughout the nineteenth and into the twentieth century. By 1920, overall daily newspaper circulation in the United States was 27.8 million, over a quarter of the U.S. population at the time. Circulation continued to rise for the next several decades, reaching a high point of 36 percent of the population by 1946.[2] At mid-century, print news was most definitely a big, profitable business. Then came the decline. It was slow at first, with circulation staying in the low to mid 30 percent range until the early 1970s, but after that things got increasingly bad. This was due in large part to the growth of television and, after that, the Internet. By 1980, only 27 percent of Americans read newspapers, a figure that just kept on falling: from 25 percent in 1990 to 20 percent in 2000, and all the way down to 14 percent in 2010. There are still a lot of daily newspapers in the United States—over 900 at last count—and their overall circulation is an impressive-sounding 43 million. But this represents a steep decline from the glory days of newspapers.

## THE BIG THREE OF PRINT (AND USA TODAY)

At the epicenter of the print news universe is the New York Times. Founded in 1851, the Times is owned by the New York Times Company, which also owns 17 other papers, including the International Herald Tribune and the Boston Globe. The Times, which caters to both a large New York metropolitan area audience and the country as a whole, is widely regarded as the "newspaper of record" for the United States. It has consistently earned high praise in journalistic circles, winning over 100 Pulitzer Prizes (U.S. journalism's highest honor), far more than any other U.S. newspaper. Behind its reporting is a newsroom staff of 1,250 people, also far more than any other U.S. newspaper.[3] A lot of people read the Times: its average circulation is 1.6 million on weekdays and over 2 million for the hefty Sunday edition. While the basic news reporting at the Times may be fairly straightforward, its editorial and opinion pages are definitely left of center ideologically, as demonstrated by the papers' record of presidential endorsements: the last Republican the Times endorsed was Dwight Eisenhower, in 1956.[4]

The New York Times may be the paper of record, but it's not the largest U.S. newspaper, a title that goes to the Wall Street Journal, with its average daily circulation of 2.1 million.[5] The paper, founded in 1889 by Dow

Jones & Company, publishes Monday through Saturday and focuses primarily on business and economic news, though it also provides significant coverage of politics, particularly on issues that are economic in nature (which a lot of political issues are). In recent years it has increased its political reporting as part of a larger effort to capture some of the *New York Times*'s readership. The *Journal* is generally seen as ideologically conservative, and since 2007 it has been owned by Rupert Murdoch's News Corp, which controls a number of other conservative media outlets, most notably Fox News.* The paper's conservative orientation is reflected in its editorial-page philosophy, which "stands for free trade and sound money; against confiscatory taxation and the ukases† of kings and other collectivists; and for individual autonomy against dictators, bullies, and even the tempers of momentary majorities."[6] Its news coverage is highly regarded, as demonstrated by the 34 Pulitzer Prizes the paper has won over the years. The *Journal*'s newsroom staff of 700, while far smaller than that of the *New York Times*, is larger than any other newspaper's.[7]

The *Washington Post* isn't exactly a national newspaper, but because its local news comes out of Washington, D.C., it features plenty of national political reporting. The *Post* has been regularly recognized for journalistic excellence, winning 57 Pulitzer Prizes, more than any paper except the *New York Times*. The *Post* has a large newsroom, but at 600 people it's noticeably smaller than that of the *Wall Street Journal* and less than half the size of the *New York Times* newsroom staff.[8] By weekday circulation it only ranks eighth in the country, averaging slightly over half a million copies sold every day, but the *Post*'s readers are among the most powerful people in politics, giving the paper an influence far greater than what the circulation numbers might suggest. The *Post* has been publishing since 1877 and is owned by the Washington Post Company, which also owns several small newspapers, a handful of TV stations, and the Kaplan educational services company. Until 2010, the Washington Post Company also owned the weekly newsmagazine *Newsweek*. Like the *New York Times*, it's often seen as left of center politically, though its op-ed page generally offers more room for conservative voices than the *Times* does.

Although *USA Today*'s daily circulation of 1.8 million puts it second only to the *Wall Street Journal*, it has never been a major force in national political news. The paper, which was founded in 1982 by the Gannett media conglomerate (owner of over 90 daily newspapers and 23 television stations), was designed to specifically target television viewers by

---

*The *Journal* stopped making presidential endorsements after picking Herbert Hoover in 1928.
†"edicts or proclamations."

featuring plenty of snappy color pictures and graphics (almost unheard of in newspapers at that time) along with shorter, easier to read articles. The paper's TV association was carried out even to its distinctive street-purchase boxes, which were designed to look like television sets. While *USA Today* has featured some strong political coverage at times, it has never been very highly regarded and has yet to win a Pulitzer Prize.

## NEWSMAGAZINES

The telegraph and the steam-powered press made it possible to get more news to more people than ever before, which seems like a really good thing. But the sheer volume of all that news could easily become overwhelming, even in those pretelevision, pre-Internet days. As one newspaperman writing in the early 1920s put it, "People are, for the most part, poorly informed. . . . News comes from a thousand fronts — politics, science, literature, business— How can a man get it all? grasp it? put it together? make it his own?"[9] The person who wrote this was Henry Luce, who in 1923 cofounded *Time*, the first weekly newsmagazine in the United States.* For the reasonable price of $1 (about $13.50 in 2012 dollars) readers across the United States could sign up to have 12 weekly editions delivered to their mailboxes. Billing his magazine as "the first and only systematic condensation of the news,"[10] Luce promised complete coverage of basically everything that mattered (even "aeronautics" and "moving pictures"), all in 26 pages, which, as Luce pointed out in early ads for *Time*, could be easily read "in the hour before dinner."[†]

The idea caught on, and the initial list of 12,000 subscribers quickly grew. By the early 1960s, *Time* could be found in over 150 countries and had 3.6 million weekly subscribers in the United States.[11] It has long been the most popular American newsmagazine and is probably best known for its "Person of the Year" issue.[‡] After a 1989 merger with Warner Communications followed by a $164 billion buyout by then Internet giant AOL in 2000, *Time* became part of the largest media conglomerate in the world.[§]

---

*Both Luce and his cofounder Briton Hadden were only 24 years old at the time. Hadden died of a streptococcus infection less than six years later (not all that uncommon in preantibiotic times) while Luce would go on to create the Time-Life publishing empire and become one of the most prominent Americans of the twentieth century.

†Demonstrating, if nothing else, that superficial news coverage existed long before cable TV and the Internet.

‡Until 1999, it was "Man of the Year," even though there had been four female Men of the Year prior to that point.

§In 2003 AOL, which had been called AOL Time Warner, was renamed Time Warner Inc. In 2009, AOL was spun off as an independent company.

*Time* remained popular even after the emergence of the Internet, and as recently as 2006 it boasted a national circulation of over 4 million.[12] But even *Time* couldn't fight the online tide forever, and its circulation began a steady decline in the later years of the decade. By mid-2012, *Time* was down to 3.27 million subscribers, a major drop from even a few years before, though still enough to place *Time* in the top 10 of all magazines in the United States and way ahead of any other newsmagazine.[13] *Time* has had an online presence since 1993, but the magazine's website has never had anywhere near the popularity or impact of the print version.

The early success of *Time* didn't go unnoticed in the publishing world, and it wasn't long before a competitor emerged. In 1933 former *Time* editor Thomas Martyn founded *Newsweek* in the belief that "*Time* is too inaccurate, too superficial, too flippant and imitative."[14] *Newsweek* floundered for a few years, but a relaunch in 1937 soon boosted the magazine's circulation to over a million, giving *Time* its first legitimate competition. *Newsweek* continued to prosper, reaching over 3 million subscribers by the 1980s, but it's never been able to match the success of *Time*. And while *Time*'s subscriber base gradually fell away starting in the mid-2000s, *Newsweek* dropped off a cliff, with the magazine losing nearly half of its subscribers between 2007 and 2012.[15] In 2010, the *Washington Post*, which had owned *Newsweek* since 1961, sold the magazine to 91-year-old billionaire Sidney Harman for the much-publicized price $1, though in addition to paying that dollar, Harmon had to take on *Newsweek*'s outstanding debt—somewhere in the neighborhood of $70 million.[16] Later that year, *Newsweek* agreed to a merger with the website *The Daily Beast* to form the (awkwardly named) Newsweek Daily Beast Company. Although *Newsweek* maintained a circulation of over 1.5 million, making it the second most popular newsmagazine in the United States, in late 2012 Editor-in-Chief Tina Brown, citing the "challenging print advertising environment," announced that the magazine would be going all-digital in 2013, with the last print edition being the December 31 issue.[17]

*Time* and *Newsweek* have dominated the newsmagazine business for decades, but several other publications have managed to carve out niches by appealing to smaller, but wealthier and more influential, audiences. The closest thing to a direct competitor to *Time* and *Newsweek* is *The Economist*, a British newsweekly. Although the focus of *The Economist* is international news, its strong coverage of U.S. politics and economics has made it a favorite of opinion-makers in the United States. In sharp contrast to *Time* and *Newsweek*, *The Economist*'s circulation numbers have been great: it's more than doubled its subscriber base over the last decade—a truly impressive feat considering how circulation numbers in the magazine industry have nosedived—and now has nearly 850,000 sub-scribers.[18] Political news coverage in *The Economist* is almost always more substantive than what you're likely to find in *Time* or *Newsweek*, something that appeals to the highly-educated audience the magazine attracts. Most impressively, *The Economist* has managed to add subscribers with a premium-pricing model, charging over three times as much as either *Time* or *Newsweek*.[19]

There are only a few other major weekly newsmagazines that devote any substantial space to politics. *Bloomberg Businessweek*, with a circulation of nearly a million, is the largest of them. As the title suggests, the main focus of the magazine is business, though since its 2010 relaunch and renaming after being acquired by billionaire New York mayor Michael Bloomberg (who added the "Bloomberg" to what had formerly been just plain old *Businessweek*) the magazine has increased its political coverage.

The magazine *The Week* has prospered by taking a different approach than its competitors. It's almost exclusively a news aggregator, providing quick and easy summaries of the week's major stories in politics, business, the arts, and science. The magazine, which was founded in the United Kingdom in 1995, started publishing a U.S. edition in 2001 and has increased its paid circulation every year to a current level of over half a million subscribers despite a generally disastrous market for print magazines.[20]

There are also a number of weekly political magazines with a clear ideological agenda. Their focus tends to be less on the latest news and more on analysis and opinion. The most popular conservative political magazines are *National Review* and *Newsmax*, with the two main liberal weekly magazines being *The Nation* and *The New Republic*. These magazines don't have nearly the subscriber base of their less blatantly ideological competitors—*Newsmax*, the most popular of them, has a paid circulation of less than 200,000.[21] While the audiences for these magazines are relatively small, their readers are many of the most involved and influential people in politics, giving them a political voice louder than the circulation numbers alone would suggest.

## POLITICS ON THE RADIO

The technology that made radio possible was developed in the late nineteenth century, making radio the first broadcast media. As with many new technologies, it took a while for radio to become a viable consumer product, and it wasn't until the 1920s that the commercial stations appeared. In 1920, New York's KDKA became the first licensed station to broadcast election results, reporting on Republican Warren Harding's presidential victory over Democratic candidate James Cox.[22] In 1926 the National Broadcasting Corporation (NBC) became the first national radio network, consisting of a "Red Network" featuring entertainment programming and a "Blue Network" for news. The Columbia Broadcasting System (CBS) followed in 1927. (ABC, the third major network, wouldn't be around until 1945). While the ever-growing number of radio stations increased coverage of politics throughout the 1920s, it wasn't until the following decade that there would be regular news broadcasts on radio.

In its first few decades, the growth of radio was explosive. In 1922, when the Census Bureau first started keeping track of radio ownership, there were only 60,000 U.S. households with radio sets.[23] Two years later, the figure had jumped to over 2 million, and just over a decade after that, President Roosevelt would be giving his "fireside chats" to a U.S. radio audience of nearly 20 million people. By the beginning of World War II radio was nearly everywhere, with over 80 percent of all U.S. homes owning a set.* Soon after the war ended, commercial television came along, but radio prospered even in the face of this competition, reaching over 90 percent of all U.S. homes by 1950. Radio was now virtually everywhere, making it the unquestionable king of broadcast media.

But radio's dominance wouldn't last long: starting in the 1960s, more and more Americans would turn to television, both for news and entertainment. Radio was still enormously popular, but it couldn't compete with the visual appeal of television, a mismatch that only increased as TV sets became larger, less expensive, and able to broadcast in color. You can still find political news in modern radio, but it's been a long time since radio posed any real threat to television in that area. Although radio has largely ceded "straight news" reporting to television and newspapers, it's been able to develop an enormously popular news niche of its very own: political talk.

Blowhards and know-it-alls have always been part of politics on the radio, but it wasn't until the 1990s that the highly inflammatory political talk format millions of Americans have come to know and love (or hate) really came into its own. This happened because of two major actions of the federal government. The first was the Federal Communication Commission's 1987 decision to repeal its Fairness Doctrine, which required that broadcast networks present balanced presentation of public issues. The rule was created in 1949, a time when the public had far fewer news choices. But since then the number of broadcast news options had grown

---

*And while you can pick up a radio for next to nothing today, back then radios were major consumer purchases. A 1938 Westinghouse Presto-Matic set would run you $74.50, the equivalent of over $1,200 today.

large enough that the FCC felt the public could receive balanced coverage without the federal government placing a coverage mandate on privately-owned broadcasters. When the rule was in effect, it meant that for every left-wing rant, you had to present a right-wing rant—not the sort of programming that would appeal to either the left or the right. Once the rule was rescinded, stations could openly appeal to partisan political audiences with openly biased programming.

The second b government action was the passage of the Telecommunications Act of 1996, which removed many previously existing barriers to ownership of multiple radio stations. The relaxed ownership rules allowed huge corporations like Clear Channel to buy up hundreds of radio stations across the country. The new corporate owners quickly went to work finding ways to maximize profits in an industry that, to that point, had been dominated by thousands of small station owners. The new owners ran the numbers and came to the conclusion that playing music on the radio wasn't such a great way to make money anymore because millions of people were abandoning the annoying commercials and limited playlists of music radio for MP3s, Internet radio, and music streaming services. They also realized that talk could be far more lucrative than music: call-in shows were more interactive than music programming, there was less competition from new technology, and (best of all) the people who listened to talk radio were, on average, wealthier than music listeners, making them more attractive to advertisers. Nationwide audiences made it possible for these media giants to syndicate one program to hundreds of stations across the country and attract deep-pocketed national advertisers.

Political talk was perfect for this new environment because national politics is as relevant in Alabama as it is in Arizona. Better yet, there were tens of millions of people with strong views about politics; people who would be eager to hear about the latest outrages of their political opponents. It was like sports radio but even better: a lot more fans, and almost all of them devoted to one of two teams.

But only one of those teams really showed up. Politics on the radio is pretty much *conservative* politics, as you can see in Table 2.1, which lists the top-rated talk radio shows in 2011. Strongly conservative shows are the clear majority overall, as well as making up 7 of the top 10.* And while many conservatives will claim to the last breath that public radio is intensely liberal, the two National Public Radio (NPR) shows that crack the top 10 spend far less of their time on partisan rhetoric than any of the

---

*That's counting libertarian as conservative. On most of the big political issues of the day—particularly economic issues—there's not too much difference between the two.

## Table 2.1.   Top-Rated Talk Radio Shows (2011)

| Rank | Show | Type | Avg. Audience (millions) |
|---|---|---|---|
| 1 | Rush Limbaugh | Conservative talk | 15 |
| 2 | Sean Hannity | Conservative talk | 14 |
| 3 | Morning Edition | Public Radio News | 12.96 |
| 4 | All Things Considered | Public Radio News / Talk | 12.27 |
| 5 | Michael Savage | Conservative talk | 9 |
| 6 | Glenn Beck | Conservative talk | 8.5 |
| 6 | Mark Levin | Conservative talk | 8.5 |
| 8 | Neal Boortz | Libertarian talk | 6 |
| 8 | Laura Ingraham | Conservative talk | 6 |
| 10 | Weekend Edition | Public news/ talk | 5.12 |
| 11 | Jim Bohannon | Moderate talk | 3.75 |
| 11 | Jerry Doyle | Libertarian talk | 3.75 |
| 11 | Mike Gallagher | Conservative talk | 3.75 |
| 11 | Michael Medved | Conservative talk | 3.75 |
| 11 | Doug Stephan | Liberal talk | 3.75 |
| 16 | Bill Bennett | Conservative talk | 3.5 |
| 17 | Talk of the Nation | Public radio talk | 3.39 |
| 18 | Alan Colmes | Conservative talk | 3.25 |
| 18 | Thom Hartmann | Liberal talk | 3.25 |
| 18 | Rusty Humphries | Conservative talk | 3.25 |
| 18 | Dennis Miller | Conservative talk | 3.25 |
| 18 | Stephanie Miller | Liberal talk | 3.25 |
| 18 | Ed Schultz | Liberal talk | 3.25 |
| 24 | Don Imus | Moderate talk | 2.25 |
| 25 | Hugh Hewitt | Conservative talk | 1.75 |

*Source:* Ratings data from "Talkers.com—'The Bible of Talk Radio and the New Talk Media,'" n.d., http://www.talkers.com/top-talk-radio-audiences/. Talkers does not list NPR ratings data, which was taken from "Audience Estimates: NPR," NPR.org, http://www.npr.org/templates/archives/archive.php?thingId=125885971.

conservative shows on the list. There are only two in-your-face liberal shows on the list—Stephanie Miller and Ed Schultz—and they're down toward the bottom, with audiences a fraction of the size of conservative talk radio kings Rush Limbaugh and Sean Hannity.

There are two popular theories as to why conservatives dominate political talk. Ask a liberal, and the story you'll probably hear is that talk radio deals in mostly incoherent, illogical outrage, and liberals are far too calm and rational to buy in to such nonsense. Conservatives are more likely to argue that because the national television networks, two of the three main national papers, and NPR are driven by liberal agendas, conservatives had no choice but to seek out their own media outlets. Accusations of liberal bias in the mainstream media (MSM) are common on conservative talk shows, and whether these accusations are true or not, they're smart business: convincing your audience that you're the only one they can trust for their news is a great way to lock in your customer base. Judging by the gargantuan salaries the top talk-radio hosts are making, the strategy is paying off handsomely: Rush Limbaugh has an eight-year, $400 million dollar radio contract, with second-ranked talk-radio host Sean Hannity getting a $100 million, five-year deal (which doesn't include his television work for the conservative Fox News).[24,25]

Whether conservative or (occasionally) liberal, almost all of the top politics shows on radio have a common approach. They don't bother with news gathering or reporting, a resource-intensive job they leave to newspapers and television networks. The job of the political radio host is considerably easier (and more fun): getting listeners very upset at whatever awful thing those evil geniuses/clueless fools in the opposition are doing. It's a successful business model, but although screeching condemnation and wild accusation may be entertaining radio, it makes for pretty lousy, gridlocked politics.

## TV NEWS

The history of TV news is a lot shorter than that of print because while we've had the tools to mass produce newspapers for over 500 years, the technology behind television broadcasts has only been around since the 1920s. It took a while for TV to appear in people's living rooms, with regular national network broadcasts not beginning until the late 1940s. By 1955, the year the Census Bureau first began gathering data on TV ownership, 67 percent of households in the United States had sets, a figure that would rise to 88 percent by 1960.[26] The pervasive impact of television news was seen most clearly in the aftermath of the 1963 assassination of President Kennedy, when an estimated 96 percent of all Americans watched televised coverage of the funeral.[27] By the end of the 1960s, nearly every home in the country had at least one television, and TV had become Americans' number one source for news, a position it still holds today.

TV news broadcasts are just about as old as network television itself, with NBC and CBS beginning 15-minute national news shows in 1948 and ABC following suit five years later. A decade passed before network news switched to the current half-hour length on two of the three networks: once again, ABC brought up the rear, not going to 30 minutes of nightly news until 1968. It was during this time, often referred to as the Golden Age of TV news, that the first celebrity news anchors began to appear. The most notable of them were Edward R. Murrow and Walter Cronkite, both of whom made their names as overseas radio correspondents during World War II. The three networks had a virtual monopoly on TV news until another technology—cable television—allowed the networks' dominance to be challenged. In 1980, when CNN, the first all-news network, was founded, fewer than 20 percent of all U.S. households had cable. Congress's deregulation of cable rates in the Cable Communications Act of 1984 was a major force behind the growth of cable, and by 1990 over half of all U.S. households had cable service. The greater reach of cable TV led to the founding of two more cable news networks, Fox News and MSNBC, both of which began operation in 1996. By 2000, two-thirds of U.S. houses had a cable TV subscription, a number that has remained relatively stable ever since.[28]

## NETWORK NEWS STILL RULES

Although cable news ended the networks' monopoly on TV news, ABC, NBC, and CBS still attract substantially more news viewers than their cable competitors. Overall audience size comparisons are imperfect because the three networks air 30-minute news shows from 6:30 to 7:00 PM while the cable channels offer a multitude of shows 24/7. However, one way of getting a sense of the disparity in audience size is to compare the average number of viewers of the network news shows to the average primetime audience of the cable channels. In 2011, 22.5 million people watched one of the network news shows on an average night, compared to only 3.3 million primetime cable news viewers—only 14 percent the size of the network news audience.[29] NBC's *Nightly News* is the leader of the network pack, with an average audience of 8.75 million, followed by ABC's *World News* at 7.82 million and CBS's *Evening News* at 5.97 million. Network news features very little opinion and editorial content and so is generally thought to be less ideologically biased than the major newspapers, all of which devote significant space to editorials and opinion pieces.

The top two cable news networks have essentially abandoned a middle-of-the-road approach to news in favor of clearly partisan takes on political reporting. This is a good business move, as it means that they aren't really competing with network news shows and can instead carve out their own smaller, but still substantial, audiences. Fox News has been especially successful with this approach, which has kept it on top of the cable news ratings for many years. In 2011, Fox averaged 1.9 million viewers in prime time, with its number one show, *The O'Reilly Factor*, drawing an average audience of 2.96 million viewers per night.[30] MSNBC, the number two cable network, has taken the Fox approach and applied it with a left-of-center twist. This helped to move it past CNN in the cable newsratings, though MSNBC's audience is still only 40 percent the size of Fox's. In 2011, MSNBC averaged 773,000 viewers in prime time, with the top MSNBC show, *The Rachel Maddow Show*, attracting 983,000 viewers per night. CNN is the only one of the three cable networks to not embrace a partisan approach, and not coincidentally it trails the pack with an average audience of 650,500 in prime time. Its highest rated show—*Anderson Cooper 360*—drew an average of 770,000 viewers per night in 2011.

## "FAKE NEWS"

1996 was an important year for cable news. As we've already seen, this was the year that both Fox and MSNBC started broadcasting. But it was also the year the current cable "news" ratings king began broadcasting—Comedy Central's *Daily Show*.

*The Daily Show*, which airs Monday through Thursday at 11:00 PM, isn't exactly a news show. In fact, according to Jon Stewart, who has hosted the show since 1999, it's "Fake News" that satirizes politics and the media as opposed to reporting on them. Although it's been suggested that many *Daily Show* viewers get their political news largely from the show, a report by the Project for Excellence in Journalism, which analyzed an entire year of the show, found that *The Daily Show* "not only assumes, but even requires, previous and significant knowledge of the news on the part of viewers if they want to get the joke."[31] (Though some of this previous knowledge may come from repeated viewing of *the Daily Show* itself, as opposed to other sources of political news.)

Fake News has proven to be awfully popular, as *The Daily Show*'s ratings demonstrate. In 2011, *The Daily Show* averaged 2.3 million viewers per episode, a total second only to Fox's *O'Reilly Factor*. One of the show's most popular "correspondents," Stephen Colbert, was given his own show, which in 2005 started airing in the 11:30 time slot immediately after *The Daily Show*. The general format of the two shows is similar—the first part consisting of "news," followed by an interview in the second part—but the shows take decidedly different comic approaches to the news. Stewart tends to wear his cynicism on his sleeve, and his take on the news is usually much more congenial to Democrats than Republicans. Colbert does the news in the character of a conservative, know-it-all egomaniac roughly modeled after Fox's Bill O'Reilly (who Colbert mock-reverentially refers to as "Papa Bear"). His over-the-top conservative rants are done with tongue firmly in cheek and are not particularly appreciated by most die-hard Republicans. Colbert's show has also been a ratings success, averaging 1.5 million viewers per episode in 2011, more than anything offered by either MSNBC or CNN.[32]

Hoping to capitalize on the popularity of Fake News, Fox launched its own entry into the genre in 2007. *The ½ Hour News Hour* was intended to be a satirical take on the news in much the same vein as *The Daily Show*, but from a conservative perspective. As the show's creator, Joel Surnow, observed at the time, "There really is nothing out there for those who want satire that tilts right."[33] The show, which aired Sundays at 10:00 PM, received massive critical scorn—its average score from the review aggregator site Metacritic was 12 (that's out of 100), making it the lowest rated show in Metacritc's enormous database (below such gems as "The Real Wedding Crashers" and the "Knight Rider" remake)[34]. But despite the negative reviews, the show had strong initial ratings, attracting an audience of 1.5 million viewers. But the numbers plummeted quickly, and the show was cancelled after seven months and only 17 episodes. Conservatives may dominate political talk, but in the area of Fake News, they haven't been able to compete with Stewart and Colbert.

## TWENTY-FIRST CENTURY NEWS: ONLINE MEDIA

Although the technology behind the Internet has been around since the 1960s, the Internet as we know it came along considerably later. While there wasn't any one point when we suddenly "had the Internet," it's reasonable to date what most of us think of as the Internet from 1993, when the first graphical web browser—NCSA Mosaic—was released. By 1996, 19 percent of Americans were online and nearly every major national news organization has some sort of Internet presence.[35] The percentage of Americans going online continued to surge, hitting 50 percent in 2001 and reaching just over 77 percent in 2010.[36] Back in the early days, if you wanted to go online, you had to use a phone line to dial in to a service provider every day, and connections were frustratingly slow and not infrequently dropped. This made for an inefficient and frequently irritating online experience. In 2000, only 6.8 million Americans had fast, always-on broadband connections, but over the course of the decade the number of people with high-speed access rose rapidly. Today, over 80 million people have broadband access, which has transformed the Internet from slow and annoying to the easiest and most convenient way to get news.[37]

**Table 2.2.   Top News Sites: Average Monthly Unique Visitors, 2011**

| | Site | Visitors (millions) | Category |
|---|---|---|---|
| 1 | Yahoo News | 85.9 | Internet |
| 2 | CNN Digital Network | 72.8 | TV |
| 3 | Huffington Post Media | 55.8 | Internet |
| 4 | MSNBC Digital Network | 52.7 | TV |
| 5 | New York Times | 33.2 | Newspaper |
| 6 | Tribune Newspapers | 27.7 | Newspaper |
| 7 | Fox News Digital Network | 25.5 | TV |
| 8 | ABC News Digital Network | 22.8 | TV |
| 9 | CBS News | 19.9 | TV |
| 10 | Advance Digital | 18.3 | Newspaper |
| 11 | Washingtonpost.com | 17.9 | Newspaper |
| 12 | Mail Online | 15.8 | Newspaper |
| 13 | Hearst Newspapers | 14.8 | Newspaper |
| 14 | Wall Street Journal Online | 14.6 | Newspaper |
| 15 | McClatchy Corporation | 13.6 | Newspaper |
| 16 | MediaNews Group | 12.7 | Newspaper |
| 17 | Examiner.com Sites | 11.4 | Newspaper |
| 18 | BBC | 11.2 | TV |
| 19 | NYDailynews.com | 10.6 | Newspaper |
| 20 | Guardian.co.uk | 9.8 | Newspaper |
| 21 | Belo | 6.1 | TV |
| 22 | Slate | 7.8 | Internet |
| 23 | Topix | 7.7 | Internet |
| 24 | Boston.com | 6.2 | Newspaper |
| 25 | NYPost.com | 6.2 | Newspaper |

*Source:* Kenny Olmstead, Jane Sasseen, Amy Mitchell, and Tom Rosenstiel, "By the Numbers," Pew Research Center's Project for Excellence in Journalism, http://stateofthemedia.org/2012/digital-news-gains-audience-but-loses-more-ground-in-chase-for-revenue/digital-by-the-numbers/.

While the Internet has made it possible for almost anyone with a computer and a connection to report or analyze politics, online news is still dominated mainly by old-media companies, as Table 2.2 shows. The online arms of newspapers are particularly well represented, locking up 14 of the top 25 slots. Although television-based content providers only have half as many slots, they're nearly equal to online newspapers in terms of Top 25 audience share, at 36 percent.

This still leaves new media with a hefty 27 percent online news audience share, which is nothing to sneeze at. But the bulk of this comes from Yahoo

News and The Huffington Post, sites that do very little original reporting, mainly aggregating news from traditional outlets and adding in opinion blogs. Yahoo!, founded in 1995, is an old-new-media company, whereas The Huffington Post, which came along a decade later, represents a newer wave of Internet news. The site's trademark features are gigantic headlines, gobs of juicy celebrity news, strongly opinionated bloggers, and a decidedly left-wing sensibility. The Huffington Post has been very aggressive in marketing, using a variety of means, some of a questionable nature, to drive traffic to its site.* But it's not all fluff: the site's reporting has received some critical praise, most recently a 2012 Pulitzer Prize for national reporting, making it the first online-only daily publication to win journalism's highest award.

## SOCIAL NEWS: THE NEW NEW MEDIA

Social media sites have attracted huge audiences in recent years. In 2011, only five years after opening access to the general public, Facebook had 880 million unique visitors, making it the most visited site on the web. Twitter, which finished the year as the 15th most popular site, had over 140 million active users, who sent out a billion tweets every three days.[38] Facebook and Twitter don't employ a single reporter or opinion columnist, and their basic design prevents them from being news sources—tiny text boxes and 140-character-limit tweets make it virtually impossible to use them for actual reporting. But despite all this, they are a large and growing force in online news simply because of the sheer volume of traffic they direct to news sites. While only a small fraction of Facebook posts or Twitter tweets includes a news link, even small fractions are a big deal with that many users. In 2011, 8.6 percent of all traffic to news sites came from a link on a social media site, a figure that represents a 57 percent increase over 2009. [39] Nearly all news organizations have Facebook pages and multiple Twitter feeds (169 of them at the *New York Times*[40]) in an attempt to drive as much traffic as possible to their websites. While neither Twitter nor Facebook can keep on growing as quickly as they have over the past few years, in the near future their numbers, as well as their impact on traditional news media, should continue to grow.

## MORE NEWS ISN'T BETTER NEWS

For political news addicts, it's a great time to be alive. There have never been more ways to get the news, which is now available instantly no

---

*The most (in) famous example of this is its "What Time Is the Super Bowl?" headline, written specifically to generate the maximum number of hits from search engines.

matter where you are (as long as you've got wi-fi or cell reception). It would be nice to think that easier access to political news means a more informed public, but this doesn't seem to be the case. A Pew Research Center study that looked at changes in political knowledge from 1989 through 2007 found that the massive increase in news options during that period had little impact on Americans' political knowledge. Then, as now, many of us can identify top leaders and remember the vague outlines of current political stories, but that's about it. There's been no measurable increase in our generally dismal ability to understand—or even remember—what's beyond the headlines.

How is this possible? The main reason why more political news doesn't mean greater political understanding is that where you get your political news matters—much more and in many more ways than most people realize. We'll be looking at these differences in the next chapter.

## NOTES

1. Alex Jones, *Losing the News: The Future of the News That Feeds Democracy* Reprint, New York: Oxford University Press, 2011, p. 85.

2. Pre-1940 circulation data from Benjamin M. Compaine and Douglas Gomery, "Who Owns the Media? Competition and Concentration in the Mass Media Industry," 3rd ed. (Mahwah, NJ: Routledge, 2000). Post-1940 circulation data from "Newspaper Circulation Volume," Newspaper Association of America, accessed December 21, 2012, http://www.naa.org/Trends-and-Numbers/Circulation/Newspaper-Circulation-Volume.aspx.

3. David Kaplan, "NYT To Cut 20 Newsroom Jobs; Plan Calls for Buyouts, Not Layoffs," *paidContent*, October 14, 2011, http://paidcontent.org/2011/10/14/419-nyt-to-cut-20-newsroom-jobs-plan-calls-for-buyouts-not-layoffs/.

4. "New York Times Endorsements through the Ages—Interactive Feature—NYTimes.com," New York Times, accessed December 21, 2012, http://www.nytimes.com/interactive/2008/10/23/opinion/20081024-endorse.html.

5. All newspaper circulation data are averages for the six-month period from October 2011 to March 2012 as reported by the Audit Bureau of Circulations, accessed May 14, 2012, http://abcas3.accessabc.com/ccirc/newstitlesearchus.asp.

6. *Wall Street Journal*, "About Us: Our Philosophy," accessed May 14, 2012, http://online.wsj.com/article/SB126841434975761027.html.

7. Michael Baranowski, e-mail to Sara Blask, corporate communications manager for *The Wall Street Journal*, May 17, 2012.

8. Patrick B. Pexton, "What Buyouts Reveal about the Washington Post's Strategy," *The Washington Post*, February 11, 2012, Opinions, http://www.washingtonpost.com/opinions/what-buyouts-reveal-about-washington-post-strategy/2012/02/10/gIQAZ8V44Q_story.html.

9. Time Magazine advertisement in *The New Yorker*, May 16, 1925.

10. Advertisement in the *New Yorker*, May 16, 1925, p. 33.

11. "History of TIME—Archive Collection—TIME," accessed December 21, 2012, http://www.time.com/time/archive/collections/0,21428,c_time_history,00.shtml.

12. "Magazines: By the Numbers," Pew Research Center, accessed June 22, 2012, http://stateofthemedia.org/2012/magazines-are-hopes-for-tablets-overdone/magazines-by-the-numbers/.

13. "ACCESS ABC: eCirc for Consumer Magazines," accessed June 21, 2012, http://abcas3.accessabc.com/ecirc/magtitlesearch.asp.

14. Andrew Losowsky, "Review: Newsweek, Part One—The History," accessed June 22, 2012, http://www.losowsky.com/magtastic/2011/newsweek-history/.

15. "Magazines: By the Numbers," Pew Research Center, accessed June 22, 2012.

16. Rebecca Dana and Peter Lauria, "Newsweek's Hidden Problem," The Daily Beast, August 4, 2010, http://www.thedailybeast.com/articles/2010/08/04/newsweek-sales-hidden-problem-ceo-tom-ascheim.html.

17. Tina Brown and Baba Shetty, "A Turn of the Page for Newsweek," *The Daily Beast*, October 18, 2012, http://www.thedailybeast.com/articles/2012/10/18/a-turn-of-the-page-for-newsweek.html.

18. "ACCESS ABC: eCirc for Consumer Magazines," accessed June 23, 2012.

19. Subscription prices as of September 3, 2012, obtained from the respective websites.

20. "ACCESS ABC: eCirc for Consumer Magazines," accessed June 23, 2012.

21. Ibid.

22. Douglas Ferguson, "Radio News," in Wolfgang Donsbach, ed., *The International Encyclopedia of Communication* (Malden, MA: Blackwell Publishing, 2008).

23. All radio ownership data from U.S. Census Bureau, '"Historical Statistics of the United States: Colonial Times to 1970," Series F 93-105, Radio and Television Stations, Sets Produced, and Households with Sets: 1921 to 1970, http://www2.census.gov/prod2/statcomp/documents/CT1970p2-01.pdf.

24. "Rush Limbaugh: $400 Million Man," *The Huffington Post*, July 2, 2008, http://www.huffingtonpost.com/2008/07/02/rush-limbaugh-400-million_n_110417.html.

25. "Sean Hannity Gets $100 Million Deal," *The Huffington Post*, July 7, 2008, http://www.huffingtonpost.com/2008/07/21/sean-hannity-gets-100-mil_n_114026.html.

26. 1972 Statistical Abstract of the United States, Table 804: Percent of Households with Television Sets: 1955 to 1970, http://www2.census.gov/prod2/statcomp/documents/1972-01.pdf.

27. Mike Conway, "Television News," in Wolfgang Donsbach, ed., *The International Encyclopedia of Communication*, (Malden, MA: Blackwell Publishing, 2008).

28. Cable TV data from 2008 Statistical Abstract of the United States, Table 1099: Utilization of Selected Media: 1970 to 2006, http://www.census.gov/prod/2007pubs/08abstract/infocomm.pdf; and 2012 Statistical Abstract of the United States, Table 1132: Utilization and Number of Selected Media: 2000 to 2010, http://www.census.gov/compendia/statab/2012/tables/12s1132.pdf.

29. "Network by the Numbers," Pew Research Center, http://stateofthemedia .org/2012/network-news-the-pace-of-change-accelerates/network-by-the-numbers/.

30. Cable network ratings from "Cable: By the Numbers," Pew Research Center, http://stateofthemedia.org/2012/cable-cnn-ends-its-ratings-slide-fox-falls -again/cable-by-the-numbers/. Individual cable show ratings from "2011 Top Thirty Cable News Show," The Huffington Post, http://www.huffingtonpost.com/ news/2011-top-thirty-cable-news-shows.

31. Project for Excellence in Journalism. "Journalism, Satire or Just Laughs? The Daily Show with Jon Stewart, Examined," [Research report] May 8, 2008, http:// www.journalism.org/sites/journalism.org/files/Daily%20Show%20PDF_3.pdf.

32. "2011 Ratings Release," Comedy Central, accessed December 21, 2012, http://www.comedycentral.com/press/press_releases/2011/122011-2011-ratings -release.jhtml.

33. Michael Learmonth, "FNC Takes Satire Out for Spin," *Variety*, February 12, 2007, http://www.variety.com/article/VR1117959328?refCatId=14 (accessed December 20, 2012).

34. "Highest and Lowest Scoring TV Shows," Metacritic, accessed December 21, 2012, http://www.metacritic.com/browse/tv/score/metascore/all ?sort=desc&view=detailed&page=11.

35. "Poll Shows More U.S. Adults Are Going Online at Home," Wall Street Journal, May 24, 2006, http://online.wsj.com/public/article/SB1148403896782 60791-IREjYVgN_rGLeE3_6Djin1jeJZc_20070523.html?mod=rss_free.

36. "United States of America: Internet Usage and Broadband Usage Report," Internet World Stats, accessed May 23, 2012, http://www.internetworld stats.com/am/us.htm.

37. 2012 Statistical Abstract of the United States, Table 1132: Utilization and Number of Selected Media: 2000 to 2010, http://www.census.gov/ compendia/statab/2012/tables/12s1132.pdf.

38. "Twitter Turns Six," Twitter, accessed May 24, 2012, http://blog.twitter .com/2012/03/twitter-turns-six.html.

39. "Digital News," Pew Research Center, accessed May 23, 2012, http:// stateofthemedia.org/2012/digital-news-gains-audience-but-loses-more-ground-in -chase-for-revenue/.

40. http://www.nytimes.com/twitter. Count of 169 as of May 23, 2012.

# THREE

## The Medium Matters

### READING AND WATCHING

One reason why broadcast news is more popular than print is that when you're watching TV or listening to the radio you can also be doing all sorts of other things, like eating dinner, folding laundry, or driving to work (ideally not all at the same time). Broadcast news make it possible for you to multitask in a way print simply doesn't. Except it turns out that you can't really multitask. According to MIT neuroscientist Earl Miller, multitasking is largely a myth "People can't multitask very well" says Miller, "and when people say they can, they're deluding themselves."[1] What feels like multitasking to us is really our attention rapidly shifting back and forth between two (or more) things. As anyone who has tried to do multiple things at once knows, this can slow you down. Of course TV and radio don't know when we're multitasking—if doesn't matter if you're intently focused or completely distracted because the pace at which they present the news remains the same. The news about multitasking isn't all bad—because of our brain's plasticity, the more we do something the more efficient we tend to become at it. So while you can't *actually* multitask, practice will probably make you better at the task switching you're really doing when you think you're multitasking.* But this comes at a cost because the better you become at task switching, the harder it is to focus on any one thing, say researchers at

---

*Even so, *multitasking* is the term that just about everyone who studies task-switching uses. This doesn't exactly help to dispel the myth of multitasking.

Stanford University After conducting a series of experiments, they found that heavy multitaskers are more easily distracted by irrelevant stimuli, concluding that "the norm of multiple input streams will have significant consequences for learning, persuasion, and other media effects."[2] Multitasking may be a way of life in the modern world, but it's a practice that almost certainly makes it tougher for us to pay attention and carefully think through complex political issues.

It's inherently more difficult to multitask when you're reading because print media demands your attention in a way broadcast media doesn't. Any competent driver can listen to the news on a morning commute (and plenty do), but try to read a newspaper on your drive in to work and you're likely to wind up on the side of the road having learned nothing except that it's really, really dumb to try to read and drive. Even normal, non-vehicular-based reading can be challenging for the millions of people who are deficient in basic literacy skills. Although most Americans can read at some level, 14 percent are poor readers and another 29 percent can't read well enough to understand cause and effect in what they're reading, according to the National Center for Education Statistics. That's 43 percent of Americans—133 million people—who are unable to fully grasp anything but the most basic print news story.[3] But although print is more demanding, it offers a lot more than television, at least when it comes to understanding politics.

One of the most useful things about news in print is that you're in charge. If you run across a difficult concept you can slow down to take it in better, which is something readers do all the time, mostly effortlessly and unconsciously.* If there's a word or concept you're not familiar with, it's easy to stop and look it up. If you're reading the morning news and your dog starts barking at a squirrel in the yard, you can stop what you're doing, yell at the dog, and come right back to where you were, rereading the last sentence or two to get back into the flow of the article if you need to. On television you can't easily do that because the pace is set by whomever is reading the news. If they're going a little too fast for you, or you happen to miss something, you're mostly out of luck. If you have a DVR you can rewind and play back parts, but if you try to do that even a fraction as often as you do when you're reading, it will take you hours to watch a 30-minute news program. Nobody (at least no sane person) is going to do this; instead, we just move along, swept up in the flow, missing bits and pieces—sometimes important bits and pieces—along the way. As a result, people generally have better

---

*If you doubt that, try this experiment: time yourself reading a page from a popular novel and compare that to how long it takes to read an analysis of U.S. tax policy.

recall of what they've read than what they've seen. (Though some research suggests that people who are less educated, and therefore more likely to have difficulty reading, may find it easier to recall what they see on television as opposed to what they read.[4])

Editing is another important difference between print and broadcast news. Most of the news you read has been edited before it reaches you, by the author or, often times, by the author and an editor. Traditional TV and radio news is also presented from edited scripts, but a lot of the political content on TV and radio isn't traditional news. The politics you're more likely to get on broadcast media is live instant analyses, interviews, and caller questions. The immediacy of it all makes it interesting (in theory), but it's also essentially impossible to edit. Even the most quick-witted and astute analysts benefit from a bit of extra time to consider points and organize their thoughts—time that broadcast media doesn't allow them. What you're getting in broadcast news is first-draft thinking as opposed to the more polished political analysis you'd get in print.

This isn't because the people running TV and radio are necessarily doing anything wrong. The problem is deeper than that—broadcast media, by its very nature, has a hard time explaining complex things. It's just too difficult for most of the audience to hang in there and follow deep into the intricacies of a story. The ability to closely follow oral arguments is a skill that, like any other skill, needs to be developed through regular practice. Even if you're currently in school you don't get as much practice at this as you might think because between the PowerPoint your professor is probably showing, all the texting you do, and wandering thoughts related to your desperate desire to be somewhere (anywhere) else, you're mostly not trying all that hard to follow what your professor is saying. And even if you do have extraordinary focus and preternatural talent at analyzing complex spoken arguments, it would be difficult to find comprehensive, in-depth news coverage worthy of your rare gifts. The people who produce TV and radio news are paid for bringing in mass audiences, and any segment long and detailed enough to really get into a story is also likely to lose most of that mass audience.*

Another big advantage print has over broadcast news is that it's far more efficient. A comparison of a typical TV newscast and a newspaper demonstrates just how much more efficient print news is. Tuesday, May 23, 2012, was an entirely ordinary news day. That evening's NBC *Nightly News* ran for 30 minutes, as it always does, regardless of how much (or how little) newsworthy things happened that day. That evening's broadcast featured

---

*Which is the same reason why, if you're in school, your professor is probably showing you a PowerPoint or having you do small-group discussion.

11 stories, only one of which was political—results of a new presidential campaign poll. The average length of these stories was 1 minute, 47 seconds, with the longest story being a human interest piece that ran slightly over 3 minutes. While the newscast ran for 30 minutes, the stories only add up to 19 minutes and 47 seconds. The rest of the 30-minute time slot consisted of commercials and news anchor Brian Williams telling everyone what would be coming up after the commercials. In other words, over 30 percent of the news broadcast was something other than news. If you looked at a transcript of that evening's show and did some counting you'd find that the average number of words per story was 329, and that there were 3,626 words in all the stories combined.

Compare this to the *New York Times* of the next morning. (You wouldn't want to compare that day's *New York Times* because print newspapers lag a day behind in reporting the news.) The front page had six articles, three of which were political—three times as many political stories as the news broadcast. The average number of words in these articles was 1,146, or nearly 3.5 times longer than the NBC *Nightly News* stories. The total number of words of the six front-page articles combined was 6,875—almost double the total of the television stories. An average person reads at about 250 words per minute, which, if you do the math, means all six of the front page articles would take just over 27 minutes to read. For someone interested in in-depth political news, it's no contest: it makes a lot more sense to spend that half-hour with the newspaper. And for those readers who happened to have some extra time that day (or for fast readers) there were plenty of other news articles in the newspaper: 16 in the International section, 15 in National, and 22 in Business.

The comparative boringness of newspapers turns out to be another advantage, at least in terms of understanding and remembering all but the most simplistic political news. When you're reading a newspaper, there's not much else going on in the paper to compete for your attention. There will be other stories on the page, along with some pictures or graphics, and probably some ads. That's more distracting than a page with nothing but a single pictureless story, but it's a lot less distracting than a typical TV news broadcast. When you're watching the news, you receive all sorts of images that are designed to grab your attention. That makes TV more interesting than print for many people, but it also makes it harder to follow what's being said. This is especially true when news crawls—scrolling bands at the bottom of the screen with unrelated news information—are part of the news broadcast. This isn't an accident—TV is *designed* to be distracting. As media theorist Neil Postman put it,

The single most important fact about television is that people watch it, which is why it's called "television." And what they watch, and like to watch, are moving pictures—millions of them, of short duration and dynamic variety. It is in the nature of the medium that it must suppress the content of ideas in order to accommodate the requirements of visual interest; that is to say, to accommodate the values of show business.[5]

To really understand political issues, we need to pay close attention to sometimes difficult arguments, evaluate evidence, and construct and analyze complex causal chains. That's no easy job, even under the best of conditions. And when the medium is actively working against our sustained focus, as TV and radio inherently do, it can be nearly impossible.

## SO WHAT'S BROADCAST NEWS GOOD FOR?

That's not to say that TV and radio news don't have real value at times. For starters, they're the only source of news for the millions of people who can't read well enough to comfortably work their way through a newspaper or magazine. And there's no question that broadcast news can be far more convenient than print. Lots of people lead busy lives and simply don't have the time to settle in with a newspaper or an online politics site. Catching a bit of news while getting ready for work and making sure the kids get off to school may be all they really have time for. And, after all, knowing something is better than knowing nothing. That's true, but only as long as people *recognize* that they're only sort of informed. Unfortunately, this sort of self-awareness isn't all that common. There are plenty of people walking around thinking they know a whole lot more about politics than they actually do know, thanks in no small part to TV and radio. Odds are you know some of these people. You might even *be* one of these people (though odds also are that even if you are you don't realize it).

There is, however, one way in which TV news truly shines. To really understand this you need to actually experience it, which we can do (or at least simulate) with a simple experiment. First, read the below paragraph, taken from Wikipedia:

The September 11 attacks (often referred to as September 11th or 9/11) were a series of coordinated suicide attacks by al-Qaeda upon the United States on September 11, 2001. On that morning, 19 al-Qaeda terrorists hijacked four commercial passenger jet airliners. The hijackers intentionally crashed two of the airliners into the Twin Towers of the World Trade Center in New York City, killing everyone on board and many others working in the buildings. Both buildings collapsed within two hours, destroying nearby buildings and damaging others.[6]

For the second step, you'll need to be online. Go to YouTube, type in "World Trade Center Attack," and watch one of the video clips that come up in the results.

I'm betting that your emotional reaction to the video clip was a lot more intense than what you felt when reading the Wikipedia entry. For many people (myself included), the most disturbing part of the video was the point at which the second plane crashes into the tower. That's utterly transfixing TV: a jumbo jet plowing into the side of the tallest building in the biggest city of the most powerful country in the world. Yet people who spent hours glued to their televisions that day, watching those horrifying images over and over, gained less hard information than people who looked at a paper or a news website for a few minutes on September 12. This plays out in a similar, though far less intense, fashion every night on the evening news. Producers choose compelling video, which invariably means shots that have strong emotional content. The more emotionally engaged we are, the less room there is for our deliberative selves to think things through.

The strong emotional appeal of the images on television has at least one potential advantage over the far less emotionally charged print medium. People who are worked up emotionally are more likely to actually *do* something. Many people are unenthused by politics (to say the least), and a jolt of emotion can be just the thing to get them off their asses and into action. But what sort of action? Yelling "Obama is a socialist!" or "Romney hates poor people!" might make a person feel good (though probably not the same person), but intelligent, productive action has to go beyond emotions.

There have been times when the emotional power of video has undoubtedly helped to institute positive political change, like when footage of peaceful protesters being abused by authorities helped to advance the cause of civil rights in the 1960s. Unfortunately, there's no guarantee that emotional responses will lead to good things. For instance, some people (generally liberals) have suggested that the emotions roused by the images of 9/11 made it possible for the Bush administration to start a costly and unnecessary war in Iraq. Others (generally conservatives) believe that if fewer people had been entranced by how young and vibrant Barack Obama looked in comparison to John McCain, we wouldn't have had what they see as a disastrous health care reform law.

Once again, this isn't the "fault" of the people who produce television news. There's nothing inherently bad about them—it's just that their medium actively discourages complex thinking. Thinking requires considering, pausing, reflecting, understanding assumptions, checking facts, and then reconsidering—all things that take time. Doing all that on TV would result in a glacially slow pace and programs nobody would want to watch. People who are good on TV don't say things like "I'm not sure," "Hold on a minute, I need to think about that," or "Wait while I check the latest figures on that." But if you're not saying things like that, you're not thinking—you're performing.

*If you want to have a decent understanding of politics, you have to read* because television provides too little content, cut up into too many bite-sized stories. TV news can be useful, but only as an adjunct to written news. If you're getting most of your political news from TV, it's a near certainty that your view of politics is, at best, woefully incomplete.

## PAPER VERSUS SCREEN

In 2006, the online magazine *Slate* ran a story titled "I'm Canceling My Times Subscription: Why you should, too."[7] In it, media columnist Jack Shafer argued that the *New York Times*'s recent online redesign was so good that it made his expensive print subscription superfluous.* But less than a year later, Shafer fell off the "online-only" wagon and restarted daily home delivery of the *Times*. The main reason for Shafer's change of heart was his feeling that he was somehow getting less news and having more trouble remembering the news he got. This had nothing to do with the actual news the *Times* was reporting because everything Shafer would have gotten in the paper he was getting online. In fact, the *New York Times* online has *more* news coverage than the print version, which you'd naturally expect to lead to more, not less, news exposure. The reason things didn't work out the way Shafer hoped they would has a lot to do with some very subtle but extremely important differences between news on paper and news on a screen.

Very few people have given much thought to the differences between reading news on paper and reading it on a screen. It's understandable to assume that text is text, whether you're reading it on paper, a laptop, your

---

*Shafer says his print subscription cost him $621.20 per year. Subscription prices have gone down considerably since 2006, and a yearly subscription for every-day home delivery of the *Times*—which also includes online access—can be had for "only" $400 or so (as of late 2012).

phone, or a tablet. This is what media scholar Marshall McLuhan called "rear-view mirror thinking"—the assumption that new technology will more or less be an extension of what we've had in the past. History has shown that this is almost never the case, even when the new technology seems very similar to what has come before.

In his book *The Shallows*, technology writer Nicholas Carr takes a close look at the latest research on the effects of the Internet. What he finds isn't all that encouraging. Carr writes that, "Dozens of studies by psychologists, neurobiologists, educators, and Web designers point to the same conclusion: when we go online, we enter an environment that promotes cursory reading, hurried and distracted thinking, and superficial learning. It's possible to think deeply while surfing the Net, just as it's possible to think shallowly while reading a book, but that's not the type of thinking the technology encourages and rewards."[8]

One example from the growing body of scientific evidence on problems with online reading is a 2011 study conducted by researchers from the University of Oregon. Test subjects in the research were randomly assigned to two groups: the first group was given that day's *New York Times* in print and the second that got the day's *Times* on the web. Both groups were told they had 20 minutes to look over whatever stories they liked, after which they would complete a short survey. The results showed that the group reading the paper in print not only remembered more news stories than the online readers, but they remembered more *about* the stories they read.[9] This has pretty clear political implications—the less you're able to remember about what you read, the harder it's going to be for you to find connections and draw well-thought-out conclusions about any political issue.

Why is online reading so much more distracting? Part of the reason has to do with the differences between paper and screen advertising. It's really important to remember that from a business perspective the news—which you're likely to think is the main attraction of your preferred newspaper or website—only exists as a way to get you to look at ads, which are what pay the bills. One big difference between print and online advertising is that online, advertisers have a much easier time finding out what you're up to. They do this by counting web metrics like pageviews, the number of people who go to a particular web page, and clickthroughs, the number of people who click on their ad. This means that online sites can constantly fine-tune their offerings so that you look at as many pages and click on as many ads as possible. The financial incentive is for online news to offer you a bunch of short stories, spanning multiple pages, filled with links, and surrounded by eye-catching ads to distract you. Why are web articles broken into multiple pages when it would be far more convenient for readers to scroll down instead of clicking and waiting for a new page? It's because every new page is a platform for even more ads.

If you've ever logged in to a news site you've most likely given away a lot of information about yourself, information that can be used to target your interests even further. Even if you don't log in, having cookies enabled in a web browser (which most people do; they're on by default in most browsers) helps to steer certain types of ads your way. And even if you're being extra cautious, news sites can determine the general area you're in based on the IP address of your computer and serve up ads designed to appeal more to people who live where you're at. It all adds up to what media companies call a "more personalized experience." Another way of putting it is "more and better distractions."

This matters for at least two reasons. First, if you click on a link when reading a news story, your attention has been diverted. You are no longer focused on the original story and you're not likely to comprehend as much as someone who wasn't distracted by that intriguing link. Second, even if you open links in the background to look at later, or you don't click on any links at all, you're *still* being distracted. When you see a link, your brain registers it as a link, meaning that your attention is momentarily diverted, even if you choose to not take the bait and click on it. String enough of these diversions together and you end up with less overall comprehension. Newspapers and other nonelectronic media don't have links, and so they don't have this problem. As Carr puts it, "The Net is, by design, an interruption system, a machine geared for dividing attention."[10]

Differences in reading surfaces also matter. It has been suggested that the simple physicality of paper on ink matters, and that there's something about reading from a page of print that makes the experience more immersive. But even if you don't buy that difficult-to-prove argument, there's the simple fact that screens can't match the resolution of text on paper. Poorer resolution means that people read from screens more slowly than they read on paper, and they're more likely to quickly scan what they're reading, frequently not bothering to scroll down for more of a story. Over time, there's no question that screens have gotten easier to read, with the best of them rivaling newsprint for sharpness. But until the average screen looks like an iPad3 (without glare issues), old-fashioned newsprint will be duller but easier to read.

This isn't just theoretical speculation. Jakob Nielsen, one of the world's leading web usability consultants, has for years been researching how people read online. Nielsen summarizes his findings by writing, "We've known since our first studies of how users read on the Web that they typically don't read very much. Scanning text is an extremely common behavior for higher-literacy users; our recent eye tracking studies further validate this finding."[11] Scanning isn't something people only do online, but it may be more common there—a 2007 study by the Poynter Institute that compared print and online readers found that readers of print were more likely to be methodical in their reading, going through articles from beginning to end.[12]

One predictable result of our shortened attention spans is shorter news articles. The more short news articles we read, the more of a strain reading long news articles puts on us—that's the negative side of neuroplasticity. While our brains can rewire to get better at things we do on a regular basis, they also tend to dewire, making it harder for us to do things we don't get as much practice at. Anyone who's experienced "being rusty" after coming back to a sport or activity knows exactly what this feels like. Your ability to focus and pay deep attention to the news is just as liable to become rusty as your golf swing if you don't use it on a regular basis. Being rusty doesn't feel good, and the people who produce the news would rather we be just be comfortable (and keep on coming back to their sites), and so we end up with shorter stories, though at a certain point there's just not enough content for us to maintain the illusion that we're getting a full picture of what's going on, meaning that stories can't become absurdly short. But before that point is reached, we lose a lot of potentially valuable information.

This hasn't just affected online news because people used to getting their politics in smaller and smaller bites online are finding longer newspaper and magazine article harder to finish. In response, print political news is also getting shorter. On June 11, 2002, the *New York Times* featured 36 stories of more than 1,000 words. A decade later that total had dropped by nearly a quarter, to 28. The difference at the *Washington Post* was even more stark: from 29 stories of over 1,000 words to only 12, a decline of over 40 percent. A *Columbia Journalism Review* analysis of story length in the *Wall Street Journal* found much the same, with the number of 1,000-word stories declining over 20 percent from 2006 to 2011.[13]

Online reading is, by its very nature, a shallower experience than reading on paper. While there's still plenty of research to be done in this area, and online media is evolving at a rapid pace, the best available evidence we have now suggests that if you follow the news online you're likely to read and understand less than if you get your news in print. Even so, I'm not suggesting that you stop reading news online and get all your political news from traditional newspapers. I don't do that, and it would be silly to expect you to. But you might want to consider picking up a newspaper, and maybe even subscribing, even if it's just a Sunday edition. Short of that, there are a few things you can do to make your online reading less distracting. One option is to use apps that let you read online news without ads and other distractions. There are a growing number of simple and (better yet) free "distraction-free reading" apps and extensions available for all major browsers and tablets, and taking a few minutes to find and install one may go a long way toward making your online news reading more focused and effective. (You'll find some recommendations in the Appendix.)

## THE FILTER BUBBLE

One of the great things about the Internet is that it allows you to choose from a vast array of political news sources—far more than anyone could dream of a generation ago. This is also one of the big problems with politics on the Internet. Filtering through the seemingly limitless possibilities to find the perfect mix of news is a daunting task. Having lots of choices is great, but at a certain point too much of a good thing becomes a very real possibility. In his book *The Paradox of Choice*, psychologist Barry Schwartz examines the scientific research on how we react to multiple options, finding that too many choices can overwhelm us, making us feel more anxious and less satisfied with whatever we end up choosing.[14]

Can the Internet help cure the information overload it has caused? Some people think so. Clay Shirky, who studies the effects of the Internet on society, claims that the problem isn't too much information but rather what he calls "filter failure." According to Shirky, "We've had information overload in some form or other since the 1500s. What's changing now is that the filters we've used for most of that 500-year period are breaking."[15] For almost all of this time, getting news to the public was something only large, well-funded organizations could do. Back then, the news we ended up seeing was filtered by the judgment of countless editors and publishers, along with institutional rules and norms that dictated what we would see when we opened the paper or turned on the TV. In a matter of a few years, the Internet exponentially expanded the flow of information to us—by one estimate, we created more data worldwide in the last week than we did in the entire year of 2002, and the rate of increase shows no sign of slowing.[16] Almost all of this data bypasses our traditional filters because it's simply too much information for any group of humans to sort through. Unfortunately, at this point computer-based filters can't effectively handle the information flow either. Shirky believes as technology advances, filters will be better able to manage the ever-increasing torrent of information. History backs him up on this because that's exactly what's happened multiple times in the past. But it's important to remember what filters do: they keep things from us. And before we put our trust in an entirely new breed of nonhuman filters, we might want to understand exactly how they're deciding what to keep from us.

Online filters work by giving us more of what we want and less of what we don't. The more information the filter has to work with, the better it can do this job. Many filters continue to improve the longer we use them because over time a larger volume of information on our likes and dislikes is built up. This seems like a great system—the more we use it the better it gets. It is a great thing in many ways, but it comes at a high cost: the more effective a filter is, the more it shields us from ideas and viewpoints we may not agree with. Over time, it's easy to build what technology author Eli Pariser calls a "filter bubble." The more time we spend in our bubbles, the less often our views are challenged and the more sure and strident we become in our beliefs. If everyone in our virtual world is telling us that "Obama is a dangerous socialist" or that "Mitt Romney is in the pocket of the rich," we're more likely to believe it. As a result, we're less able to understand the other person's position and more likely to distrust them. And after a while, all of this mistrust might just make us more suspicious of government in general. A Pew Research Center report found that trust in government has been dropping for a decade, reaching an all-time low of 22 percent in 2010.[17] Trust in the media is also declining, but most people feel that it's *the* media that's the problem, not *their* media—in a 2011 Pew Center poll, three out of four people said that the press doesn't get the facts straight, yet 62 percent of these people believe that their chosen media do a good job reporting the facts.

If we know a filter is keeping information from us we can do something about it.* But, as Pariser notes, the online filter bubble has three unique features that makes it especially tricky to see: you're alone in it, it's invisible, and you don't choose to enter it.[18] And so even if you know that what you're seeing online is different from what someone else is seeing, it's easy to forget. Not too long ago, I Googled "Michael Baranowski," and I came up as the number-one result. This made me unreasonably happy, and I proceeded to share my happiness with all of my Facebook friends. One of them—also named Michael Baranowski (no relation)—said I was wrong, and *his* name was the number-one Google search result for "Michael Baranowski." It turns out we were both right—and both wrong.

Starting in 2009, Google began using what they call "personalized search for everyone." If you're a logged-in Google user, your search results will be based on what you've searched for and search results you've clicked

---

*Which is not to say that we *will* do something about it. Mostly we don't bother, for reasons we'll be looking at in the next few chapters.

on in the past. Even if you don't have a Google account, you'll still get results tailored to the location from which you're searching. Google doesn't know exactly where you are, but they can get a good bead on your general location from your IP address, which connects every online machine to the Internet. What this means is that a search for "Mitt Romney" will give you different results depending on who you are and where you're at. Facebook does something similar—friends whose posts you've liked or commented on in the past receive higher priority, with posts from friends you've largely ignored popping up less frequently. If your friends are posting political links—as plenty of people do—you're a lot more likely to see the links from friends who share your beliefs.

An ever-increasing percentage of the online content you see is being sur-reptitiously filtered because filtering makes good economic sense. Give people more of what they want and they'll keep coming back to your site. The better a filter gets, the more it insulates you from stuff that makes you uncomfortable. Social news, which filters what you see based on what your friends have been looking at, is increasingly popular, as seen by the success of stand-alone apps like Flipboard and Zite as well as Facebook social news integration in big news sites like the *Washington Post*. Even more common are the "personalized news" options available on just about every major political news site. There allow you to become, in effect, your own news editor, a job most of us aren't nearly as qualified for as we'd like to think. We know what we like, but filtering our politics so that we get more "good stuff" makes for problems in the real world when we inevitably have to deal with people whose filter bubbles look a lot different than ours.

## READ WIDELY

As we've seen, if you really want to become politically informed, reading is the way to go. While print lacks the allure of television, it's more efficient, and it gives you more control over your news environment than TV does. There's nothing wrong with choosing to have someone read the news to you, which is what's happening if you get your news from television. But doing the reading yourself is a lot more informative and empowering.

Regardless of what medium you get your political news from, there's always a threat of falling into a filter bubble that can narrow your vision and make it harder for you to appreciate other perspectives. Getting your news from a wide variety of sources can help a lot, but no matter how diverse your political news environment is, you're almost certain to encounter a number of systematic biases that will alter how you view politics. It's these biases that we'll take a look at in the next chapter.

## NOTES

1. "Think You're Multitasking? Think Again," NPR.org, October 2, 2008, http://www.npr.org/templates/story/story.php?storyId=95256794.

2. Eyal Ophir, Clifford Nass, and Anthony D. Wagner, "Cognitive Control in Media Multitaskers," *Proceedings of the National Academy of Sciences of the United States of America* 106, no. 37 (September 15, 2009): 15583–15587.

3. National Center for Education Statistics, "A First Look at the Literacy of America's Adults in the 21st Century," http://nces.ed.gov/NAAL/PDF/2006470.PDF.

4. Maria Elizabeth Grabe, Rasha Kamhawi, and Narine Yegiyan, "Informing Citizens: How People with Different Levels of Education Process Television, Newspaper, and Web News," *Journal of Broadcasting & Electronic Media* 53, no. 1 (2009): 90–111.

5. Neil Postman, *Amusing Ourselves to Death: Public Discourse in the Age of Show Business*, 20th Anniversary ed. (New York: Penguin, 2005), 92.

6. "September 11 Attacks," Wikipedia, accessed December 21, 2012, http://en.wikipedia.org/wiki/September_11_attacks.

7. Jack Shafer, "I'm Canceling My Times Subscription," *Slate*, April 4, 2006, http://www.slate.com/articles/news_and_politics/press_box/2006/04/im_canceling_my_times_subscription.html.

8. Nicholas Carr, *The Shallows* (New York: Norton, 2010), 115–116.

9. Arthur S. Santana, Randall Livingstone, and Yoon Cho. "Medium Matters: Newsreaders' Recall and Engagement with Online and Print Newspapers," paper presented at the annual meeting of the Association for Education in Journalism and Mass Communication, Newspaper Division, St. Louis, Missouri, August 10, 2011.

10. Carr, Nicholas. *The Shallows* (New York: Norton, 2010), 131.

11. Jakob Nielsen, 'How Little Do Users Read?' May 6, 2008, http://www.useit.com/alertbox/percent-text-read.html.

12. Poynter Institute, "EyeTrack07," accessed December 21, 2012, http://www.poynter.org/extra/Eyetrack/keys_01.html.

13. Ryan Chittum, "The Shorter-Form Journal," *Columbia Journalism Review*, October 10, 2011, http://www.cjr.org/the_audit/the_shorter-form_journal.php.

14. Barry Schwartz, *The Paradox of Choice: Why More Is Less* (New York: Harper Perennial, 2005).

15. Clay Shirky, "Web 2.0 Expo NY: Clay Shirky (shirky.com) It's Not Information Overload. It's Filter Failure," September 19, 2008, http://www.youtube.com/watch?v=LabqeJEOQyI&feature=youtube_gdata_player.

16. Klint Finley, "Was Eric Schmidt Wrong about the Historical Scale of the Internet?," *ReadWriteWeb*, February 7, 2011, http://www.readwriteweb.com/cloud/2011/02/are-we-really-creating-as-much.php.

17. "Public Trust in Government: 1958–2010," Pew Research Center, April 18, 2010, http://www.people-press.org/2010/04/18/public-trust-in-government-1958-2010/.

18. Eli Pariser, *The Filter Bubble: What the Internet Is Hiding from You* (New York: Penguin Press HC, 2011).

# FOUR

## Bias

### THE MEDIA *IS* BIASED (BUT MAYBE NOT HOW YOU THINK)

The conventional wisdom about media bias goes something like this: Bias is a bad thing, because it distorts The Truth. The media is intentionally biased, and if they really cared about The Truth/Democracy/Our Great Nation (take your pick) they would stop being biased and tell us things honestly. This conventional wisdom is almost entirely wrong. First, bias isn't necessarily bad. To be biased simply means to approach something with a predisposition. These predispositions, which can save us a considerable amount of time, are frequently based on completely reasonable information.

For instance, almost all Americans approach politics with an enormous democracy bias. Most of us are certain that government by the people is somehow just *right* and that more popular input is better than less. It isn't true in the "well, duh!" sense that $2 + 2 = 4$ is true, but for some reason we assume it to be. This bias has a significant effect on the how the media cover politics. When's the last time you remember someone in the media calling for an end to elections, or, less dramatically, simply suggesting that low voter turnout isn't necessarily such a bad thing? Even if you've never voted, you probably assume that voting is better than not voting and that there's something wrong with countries in which leaders are chosen by undemocratic methods. That's your democracy bias at work.

Not only is bias frequently useful, it's also inevitable. Even if the media wanted to, they couldn't eliminate bias because it's impossible to report on a political event without any predispositions. Everyone has political predispositions formed by countless factors: where they grew up, what their parents told them, childhood experiences, psychological makeup, and so forth. For reporters, this shows up in many ways, such as who they talk to about a story, the words they use, the tone of their voice in a broadcast, their body language—essentially every aspect of their reporting. There's no way to eliminate this because even if reporters (or their editors) take steps to consciously combat bias, they're doing it not from a position of neutrality but based on their own biases. Bias is inescapable.

Although it's impossible to eliminate bias, that doesn't mean that all versions of political reality are equally valid. Someone who really dislikes President Obama and claims that Obama said "Republicans are bad people" isn't just biased, he or she is just plain wrong.* Thankfully, outside of the "political news" you might get in some endlessly forwarded e-mail your Uncle Bob sent to everyone on his contacts list, that sort of thing doesn't usually happen. But being able to positively identify blatant falsehoods doesn't mean we can also identify the truth or even that there's a clear-cut truth to identify in the first place.

You'll be very glad to know that this is not the start of some long philosophical examination of the question "What is truth?" For our purposes, it's enough to keep in mind that politics involves a staggeringly large number of people, ideas, options, and opinions, and no single news story can hope to provide anything approaching full and comprehensive coverage of them.[†] Media can't tell the whole story because the whole story is too big to tell. You can't explain health care, or the budget, or the war in Afghanistan, or much of anything else in a minute-and-a half or 1,000 words. In that sense, *the media has to be biased* because it can never give you the whole story. This is the *single most important thing to remember about the news*.

Although some biases are so pervasive it can be tough to even see them, with a little bit of effort, many biases become visible. Once you know what to look for, it's possible to keep an eye out for bias in your news. And while your efforts to catch and adjust for bias will inevitably be imperfect, you'll be better off than most people, who take in the news unaware of the biases that affect what they read, watch, and listen to. There are plenty of biases

---

*I feel reasonably safe in assuming that, regardless of when you're reading this, President Obama hasn't said anything like that.
[†]Think of it this way. You'd probably agree that checkers is a whole lot simpler than politics. Yet that simple game has 500,000,000,000,000,000,000 possible moves.

in political media, but some are much more prevalent than others. In the rest of this chapter, we'll be looking at the worst offenders: the Seven Deadly Biases of the news.

## BIAS 1: IDEOLOGY

If you think the political news is ideologically biased, you're in good company: study after study finds that most Americans agree with you. For over a decade, polling results from the Pew Research Center have shown that a majority of Americans view the media as ideologically biased. In 2011, 63 percent saw the media as biased, the highest percentage Pew has ever recorded.[1] Political party affiliation turns out to make a big difference here: in that same poll, 76 percent of Republicans believed the media was biased, while only 54 percent of Democrats agreed. (Independents were somewhere in-between, with 63 percent believing the media is politically biased.) On the face of it, the poll results might seem contradictory. How can a majority of Republicans *and* a majority of Democrats see the media as politically biased? You might think that one of these groups has to be wrong. But in a sense, they're both right.

The reason both Republicans and Democrats can be right is that "the news media" isn't an actual thing—it's just a convenient label for all the organizations that cover the news. More importantly, nobody gets their news from "the news media." In the real world, news comes from the small number of sources we choose out of an enormous news universe. Most of us believe that *our* news does a pretty good job—it's those other parts of "the news media" that are biased. This is exactly what Public Policy Polling found in 2012 when they looked at the public's trust of specific TV news organizations. Fox News was trusted by a truly impressive 82 percent of people who considered themselves very conservative, and mistrusted by an almost equally impressive 74 percent of very liberal people. PBS, on the other hand, was trusted by only 21 percent of the very conservative, as opposed to a 76 percent trust level among the very liberal.[2] The point is that "the news media" is different things to different people depending on what they watch, read, or listen to. Trying to figure out if "the news media" is ideologically biased makes about as much sense as trying to measure how entertaining "television shows" are.

Some of the places we go for news are absolutely, unquestionably ideologically biased and make little secret of it. *National Review* is as proudly conservative as the *Huffington Post* is liberal.* Many other news

---

*Though these days, the preferred term in liberal circles is *progressive*.

organizations don't openly admit their bias but are extremely clear in signaling that they are mostly conservative or liberal. Fox News may claim to be "fair and balanced," but it's no secret that Fox presents the news with a strong conservative slant. Similarly, MSNBC, while not openly calling itself a liberal news network, is exactly that. Most traditional news organizations are considerably less obvious about it. For instance, there's general agreement that the *New York Times* is liberal in its opinion and editorial pages, but not nearly as much agreement as to whether the news reporting in the paper is ideologically biased.

Even when dealing with a single media organization, measuring the extent of ideological bias is tough. It's simple to come up with a reasonable definition of what ideological bias is: anything that seeks to promote a particular political ideology. But how exactly do you go about measuring that? For instance, if you looked at a transcript of *The Daily Show*, you'd completely miss the sarcasm in Jon Stewart's voice—sarcasm that unquestionably affects the meaning of what he says. And even if you take sarcasm into account, how do you distinguish between "a little bit of sarcasm" and "really super sarcastic"? We immediately understand the difference when we hear it, but coming up with a specific number or grade for the amount of bias being conveyed is all but impossible.

Considering all this, it's not very surprising that studies attempting to measure ideological bias in the news media end up all over the map, depending on what part of the media they look at and how they've decided to measure bias. If you'd like to think there's a conservative bias in the media, you can cite a 2012 report from the Project for Excellence in Journalism that finds more positive coverage of Mitt Romney than of President Obama.[3] If you'd prefer to believe there's a liberal bias in the media, you can refer to the work of UCLA political scientist Tim Groseclose, author of *Left Turn: How Liberal Media Bias Distorts the American Mind*.[4] Maybe you don't agree with Groseclose. That's okay too, because there are plenty of other highly regarded political scientists who think that Groseclose's research is has significant flaws.[5]

Another issue with measuring bias in political media is what I call the Cleveland Browns problem. If you were to look at coverage of the Browns over the past decade, you'd find a colossal number of negative stories. Year after year, sportswriters and analysts go on and on about how awful, incompetent, and downright pitiful the Browns' players, coaches, and management are. Is the sports media biased against the Browns? It's possible, but a far more plausible explanation for the negative Browns coverage is that the Browns have, in fact, been awful, incompetent, and downright pitiful (only 3 winning seasons in the past 20 years is downright sad). What's true for the Cleveland Browns is also true for politics—sometimes negative comments are justified due to unequivocally lousy performance. Unfortunately, politics isn't nearly as clear cut as sports, so it's a lot tougher to judge the extent to which negative political stories are justified.

None of this may matter all that much, though, because most people who care enough to follow the news already have an ideological bias and choose news sources that confirm their bias. A 2010 Pew Research Center report found that 80 percent of those who listened to conservative talk radio host Rush Limbaugh or watched Fox News' Sean Hannity were fellow conservatives, a total far surpassing the 36 percent of conservatives in the general public. The same effect holds on the other end of the political spectrum, with the proportion of liberal *New York Times* readers and MSNBC news viewers being almost double that of the population in general.[6]

There's no question that the multitude of cable news shows and the seeming infinity of web news sources has made it considerably easier for people to find news sources that confirm their biases. Mounting evidence demonstrates that this leads to an increase in the intensity of people's beliefs, which in turn moves Democrats and Republicans further apart. A 2012 Pew Research Center report finds that the difference in views between Republicans and Democrats is higher now than at any point in last 25 years.[7] This growing gap tends to push civility and cooperation to the sidelines and makes it increasingly difficult to get anything done.

If you care enough about politics to follow it on a regular basis, you are almost certainly ideologically biased. The people who produce and present your political news are *absolutely* ideologically biased. Don't think of this as a bad thing because it's not. A political ideology is actually an extremely useful way to organize and make sense of politics. It only becomes a liability when you're not aware of it in yourself and your political media. If you are aware of your ideological bias, you can seek out news sources that challenge your beliefs so that your bias won't be as likely to blind you to what's really going on.

## BIAS 2: NOVELTY

Novelty bias is the media's tendency to play up new stories. It's a bias that is fundamental to the news, which, as the name suggests, is all about what's new. This makes a lot of sense when it comes to certain types of news, where getting the latest information is particularly important. Weather is a good example: if you're planning a day at the beach, you'll definitely want to know if the latest forecast calls for a big afternoon thunderstorm. But political news is rarely like this. Try to think of a big

political story that you needed to know about right away for any other reason than to satisfy your curiosity. For most Americans, nothing comes to
mind because political news, while often important, is rarely urgent.
You may be eager to find out who won an election or what the Supreme
Court ruled on a big issue, but it makes little difference whether you find
out in a minute, a day, or even a week.

The media have a vested interest in getting us to believe that politics is
much more like the weather than it actually is. As historian John Sommerville argues, "*The only reason for making news daily is to create an information industry.* [italics in the original] You can't have a news *business* unless
you pretend that the news is daily."[8] Sommerville was writing in the late
1990s, and things have changed considerably since then. Today, the media
would like us to believe that urgent political news happens not daily but all
throughout the day. To maintain this illusion, the media must continually
come up with new stories to fill what journalists appropriately call the news
hole. The more we buy into this, the more frequently we check the news.
And more frequent news checking is better for the bottom line of media
organizations.

One reason why this bias is both really common and incredibly hard to
overcome is our basic human urge to pay more attention to new things.
According to University of Texas neuroscientist Russell Poldrack, "Novelty
is one of the most powerful signals to determine what we pay attention to in
the world. This makes a lot of sense from an evolutionary standpoint, since
we don't want to spend all of our time and energy noticing the many things
around us that don't change from day to day."[9] Being not so good at
detecting change can have disastrous consequences, and early humans who
were better at paying attention to new stuff were more likely to pass along
their genes. Our bodies encourage us to pay attention to new things by giving
us a little burst of the neurotransmitter dopamine whenever we do. Dopamine intensifies our urge to seek out more new things, and it works along
with our opioid system to give us little jolts of pleasure whenever we do.
Some psychologists believe that this chemical response may play a key role
in what's been called social media addiction—that almost irresistible urge to
check Facebook or your Twitter feed just one more time.

In the modern world there are still plenty of new things that are really
important to be aware of: miss a car that runs a stop sign and your trip to
the grocery store could land you in the ER, or worse. The consequences
for missing political news aren't anywhere close to that drastic. Unfortunately, the biological systems we've evolved to reward attention to novelty
have a hard time telling the difference between politics and an impending
car wreck. And so we're generally happy to go along with the media's

novelty bias. On the surface, it seems like everybody wins: we get those nice little dopamine hits from new political stories, journalists get their own bio-chemical fix from reporting new stories, and media companies make more money. The problem with this is that every minute we're focusing on some-thing new but relatively unimportant is a minute we're not considering something older that really matters. Because there isn't a constant stream of truly important political news, novelty bias is even more of a problem during slow political news periods, which occur throughout the year and especially in the summer months. Political journalists often refer to this time as "the silly season," when stories too trivial to make the news at other times bubble to the surface.

To truly comprehend any important political issue you have to take time to consider the historical context, evaluate the current state of affairs, and weigh the arguments for and against various proposals. This goes against our natural inclination to focus on the new—an inclination the news media does a great job of encouraging. There's no way around it: more novelty in our news means less depth. But as long as novelty sells better than depth, novelty is what will continue to dominate in the news media.

## BIAS 3: DRAMA

The old news saying "If it bleeds, it leads" captures the essence of the drama bias. In politics, where there's generally not a lot of bleeding, the drama mostly takes the form of verbal assaults. Because it draws our attention, the news media is happy to provide us with a never-ending sup-ply of political conflict. In part, that's because they're catering to our desires, but it's also because they like drama too and can easily forget that more dramatic doesn't necessarily mean more important.

This matters for several reasons. First, it means that there is less cover-age of boring but important political news. For instance, most Americans understand that government spending is enormously important, but almost nobody knows much about dull things like the mechanics of the budget process, what it means when the U.S. dollar is strong (or weak), or the relationship between unemployment and inflation. And because the news media can't get us to tune in (or stay tuned in) when we're bored, we see less coverage of this than we do of dramatic but largely unimportant sto-ries, like where President Obama was born or whether a mosque should be built a few blocks from the World Trade Center site.

Reporters can tell a story in many different ways, and our preference for drama means that they generally go with the most dramatic version. One result of this is that differences are highlighted and agreement is downplayed (which reinforces novelty bias. It's pretty common for biases to work together like this, which is one of the things that makes them so powerful). Over time, the media's conflict magnification warps our view of political reality. For example, multiple studies have found that people routinely think crime is worse than it actually is due to the media's over-emphasis on criminal activity. And in a recent analysis of health care policy reporting, reporter Steve Benen found that the two lower-court rulings overturning parts of the Affordable Care Act (a.k.a. Obamacare) received considerably more coverage than the four rulings upholding the law, which may have given the public a distorted view of judicial opinion. [10]

When naturally occurring political drama is in short supply—as it regularly is in the summer silly season—the media can do a lot to manufacture dramatic political news. Dartmouth political scientist Brendan Nyhan explored coverage of political scandals in the *Washington Post* and *New York Times* from 1977 to 2008 and found that the single most popular month for political scandals was July: right in the middle of the silly season. By Nyhan's calculation, there were over twice as many political scandals reported in July than the average for all other months. [11] This makes sense because when not much news is being made, there's still that gaping news hole to fill—and what better to fill it with than the drama of a juicy political scandal? Nyhan is not alone in making this connection; as he points out in his research, a number of other political scientists as well as journalists have noticed the link between slow news periods and increased scandal reporting. Nyhan has also found that coverage of minor gaffes by politicians—things like Obama saying "The private sector is doing fine" or Romney telling an audience "I like being able to fire people"—increases in the summer because, as he puts it, "a bored press corps with space to fill can easily lose perspective." These verbal slip-ups are political cotton candy—compelling for a moment but with a fundamental lack of substance that leaves no mark on longer-term public opinion or policy. But they're great for spicing up a slow news cycle. [12]

Over the long run, a steady stream of drama, conflict, and negativity eventually makes people see government in an undeservedly negative light. Television has led the way in this regard because dramatic footage is what TV does best. Crafty politicians (and most successful politicians are fairly crafty) understand that they can usually receive more publicity by going on the attack rather than trying to compromise; this further ratchets up the level of conflict. After a while, it's understandable if the viewing public starts to think that nobody in government can be trusted, something polling data seems to bear out. Surveys from the late 1950s—about the time television was becoming commonplace in American homes—regularly found public trust in government to be in excess of 70 percent.[13] Trust in government dropped like a rock throughout the 1960s and 1970s and never came close to regaining pre-television-era levels. A 2011 poll by CNN found trust in government to be all the way down to 15 percent, a new all-time low.[14] While many factors have surely contributed to the decline in trust over time, it's nearly inconceivable that an increasingly conflict- and drama-driven media hasn't played an important role.

A more subtle effect of the media's drama bias is that change is generally considered better than stasis. It's boring when nothing happens, and if your job is to report on stuff that does happen, you'd be understandably frustrated when there's less to report. If Congress passes a bill, it's Doing Something, which is considered a good thing. But if Congress *fails* to pass a bill, well, that's bad because it's not Doing Something. The fact that the media commonly use the extremely negative term *gridlock* to portray the lack of congressional action is a good example of this. Yet the idea that government action is always better than government inaction is just another bias, one that since at least the 1930s has become nearly as well entrenched in many Americans as their democracy bias. This is true not just for liberals, who are generally more in favor of active government, but also for conservatives, who find themselves in the ironic position of wanting a less active government but demanding big changes in policy to achieve their goal. The emergence of a truly national media during this time, and this media's penchant for promoting action because it makes for more exciting news, has almost certainly had something to do with this.

## BIAS 4: PERSONALITY

Another important media bias, one closely connected to both the drama and novelty biases, is personality bias. This is the tendency of the media to focus on people more than political institutions or processes. There are at least two good reasons why the media does this. First, people are generally a lot more interesting than institutions or processes. Second, we're able to understand people more easily than institutions or processes.* It's rare to see a national political story that isn't built around people, usually taken from a relatively small cast of recurring characters. A typical story on

---

*Or at least we *think* we understand people better. That's really the key point because even if our analysis of people is often ridiculously oversimplified, most of us generally feel a lot more comfortable with less-researched, long-distance psychoanalysis (e.g., "Obama is a privileged elite who has a deep-seated dislike of Real Americans," or "Bush was a warmonger who invaded Iraq because of his desire to show everyone that he was better than his daddy") than we do with taking a crack at something like tax policy.

the economy—almost certainly the most important policy issue of recent years—is likely to focus on what the president has (or hasn't) done to fix it, what top congressional leaders think, and what the chairman of the Federal Reserve might do rather than on the intricacies of economic policy or the institutional constraints faced by the major actors in the economic policymaking process.

This may seem to you the only way to report on the economy—if it's bad, then we need to understand what the people in charge are doing to fix it, so naturally we'll focus on them. And to an extent, that's true. This only becomes a problem when the news focuses more on "President Obama getting a win" or "Fed Chairman Bernanke calling for action" than it does on understanding the underlying issues. And when the media talks about "The Republicans" or "The Democrats" or "The American People" as if they're monolithic things (e.g., "The Republicans aren't interested in negotiating because they don't want to give Democrats any wins headed into the election. The American people are sick of all the partisan bickering"), they're essentially treating the parties as individual entities and using them to personalize the story.

From the summer of 2009 until the spring of 2010, no issue on the U.S. political scene was bigger than health care. During that time, the Obama administration was pushing for massive changes in federal health care policy that would affect nearly all Americans. With the stakes this high, you might think that coverage focusing on the state of health care in the United States and analyses of various plans would predominate. This wasn't what happened. In an analysis of the 10 months prior to the passage of the Affordable Care Act, the Project for Excellence in Journalism found that "most of the coverage focused on the politics of the bill rather than the substance of the legislation." Forty-one percent of health care stories focused on politics and strategy, nearly twice the amount of coverage devoted to descriptions of the various health care plans being proposed. Only 9 percent of the coverage investigated the current state of American health care. Trailing the pack at 8 percent was coverage of the legislative process—a process that would play a crucial role in determining the health care law that emerged.[15] It may not be the coverage we'd hope for, but it's exactly what we'd expect from a media inclined to focus much more on people than on policies.

The personality bias makes us think that individuals in government are more important than they actually are. And so when things go wrong, we have a tendency to unfairly blame the people in power. The same is true when things are going well, and the media's personalization leads us to believe that it's largely due to good leadership. For example, many people blamed President Bush for the major recession that occurred when he was in office and believe that had he been a better president, the economic crisis could have been avoided. While President Bush may be partly to blame, a thorough analysis of economic policy suggests that many of the factors that led to the recession had been put into place years, or even decades, before George W. Bush became president. But arguing "Bush's wars and insane tax cuts for the wealthy destroyed the economy!" is a lot more interesting than reviewing the implications of financial institution capital requirements put in place under the Basel II international banking accords.

We can see this bias most clearly when it comes to elections, which are the ultimate in political personalization: hundreds of one-on-one contests between Republicans and Democrats, with control of government hanging in the balance. Miles of print and thousands of hours of airtime are devoted to "horse-race" coverage of candidates and the campaigns, with ridiculously detailed analysis of every last bit of campaign strategy. Never mind that the people who study voters and elections for a living consistently find that campaigns don't really matter all that much. In fact, if you know three basic things—voters' party affiliation, whether one of the candidates is running for reelection, and the state of the economy—you can predict well over 90 percent of election outcomes. That may be reality, but it's definitely not news.

## BIAS 5: BALANCE

For many of us, balanced news coverage is fair news coverage. And fair news coverage is what everybody wants (or at least what everybody says they want). Fox News understands this well enough to use it in their motto: "Fair and Balanced." But these two concepts are actually quite different. Fairness, in the context of political news, means giving all reasonable positions the consideration they deserve. In one sense this is impossible because time and space limitations, along with the desire to constantly present new and exciting news product (novelty bias), mean that *all* reasonable positions can't be given such consideration. In the real world, the media will cover two positions. That nicely corresponds to the Democratic/liberal versus Republican/conservative storyline and also keeps things reasonably simple. Add in a third or a fourth viewpoint and things can get pretty complex, both for the journalist reporting the story and the short-attention-span audience it's intended for.

By limiting things to relatively mainstream Democratic and Republican positions, you might think that providing fair coverage is simple: just give equal time to the Democratic and Republican view of events. In other words, balance the two sides, which is exactly what many mainstream news organizations do. This would make sense if both positions had equal merit on every issue, but it's completely bizarre to think that this is usually the case. Certainly, Democrats and Republicans can come up with roughly equivalent sound bites for a story, but that's hardly the same thing as having equally defensible positions on an issue.

In response to this, you might say, "Well, it's the job of the media to present the information from both sides, and let the people figure out who's right." Again, Fox News has shrewdly tapped into this sentiment with another one of their tag lines: "We report, you decide." This might work out just fine if politics involved reasonably simple issues about which matters of fact could be fairly conclusively proven or disproven. But politics isn't like that—it's a complex series of interactions requiring considerable time and effort in order to come to any serious understanding of most issues. Most people aren't in any position to put in that sort of work. Reporters, however, *can* do this, or they can at least spend a lot of time talking to people who have devoted their lives to detailed analysis of politics and public policy.

These people are not, as a general rule, politicians. Politicians—particularly politicians still in office—can be really poor sources for political and policy information. First, their expertise isn't primarily in analyzing and understanding public policy—they hire people to do that for them. What successful politicians *are* experts at is getting people to vote for them. That's a very different thing. If getting votes means presenting an overly simplistic picture of reality, most politicians are absolutely okay with that. This is not to say that all politicians oversimplify issues. But if the public responds more to simplified than to complex issues, over time politicians who play to the public's demand for simplification will come to dominate. Second, because they care about their public image, politicians avoid saying things they believe are true if those things might hurt their electoral prospects. And unfortunately, the reverse is also sometimes true: politicians say things they don't believe if saying them will help them get more votes.

On many issues, it turns out that the weight of truly expert opinion does tilt decidedly one way or another.* When this happens, *balance* requires that both sides are presented more or less equally, but *fairness* says that the more fully supported position should be acknowledged as such. But all too often, that doesn't happen. As media scholar Marvin Kaplan puts

---

*Expert opinion has gotten a bum rap in recent times, generally by people who profess a profound distrust of those they derisively term elites.

it, "Instead of trying to tell us what's true, journalism now prides itself on finding two sides to every story, no matter how feeble one side may be. There's no grand narrative making sense of the progression of current events; there are just dueling narratives, competing story lines, alternate and equally plausible ways to connect the dots."[16]

The reason why balance often wins out over fairness is simple: balance is easier. Fairness requires a lot more work because to be fair, a reporter has to take the time to find out if the weight of informed opinion tilts in a particular direction. It's simpler to just call someone from one side, get a few quotes, call someone from another side for a few more quotes, and move on to the next new thing. That doesn't mean reporters are lazy—there's no credible evidence that they work any less hard than other Americans. But there's always more news product to churn out, and reporters who can't meet their production quotas aren't likely to be reporters for very long.

## BIAS 6: SPEED

The news media has undergone enormous changes in the last three decades. The most obvious change is that there are far, far more choices. In 1980, there was only one cable news network and no Internet.* The news options available to the average American were very limited: three national networks and their half-hour news broadcasts, which had to be watched live because there were no DVRs (and programming a VCR—if you even had one—was a colossal pain). Aside from that, there was news coverage on the radio, along with the local paper. If you were a little more into news, you might subscribe to the *New York Times* or the *Wall Street Journal* (*USA Today* wouldn't be around for a few more years) and get a weekly news magazine, probably *Time* or *Newsweek*.

As cable television grew, the news choices available to consumers greatly expanded, and with the emergence of the Internet in the mid-1990s, the number of news sources soared. The explosion of choice has been a good thing in many ways, not the least of which is the far greater convenience of being able to get news whenever you want. For people who love following politics, this has been a golden age—never has so much information been so readily available.

There's a downside to this plenitude. We've already seen how too many options can be overwhelming, both to us and the filters we use to manage all

---

*Technically, there was an Internet, but it was a tiny, text-based thing that only a very small group of scientists used to exchange messages. There wouldn't be a proper Internet until the mid-1990s.

of our news options. Then there's the related danger of our filters giving us what we want but not what we need to be informed citizens. In addition to all this, more choices for us means more competition for news organizations. Because news has to be new, a big part of that competition focuses on who can get the story first. Before cable news and the Internet, the production schedule of the news was essentially set: the morning papers would all come out at the start of the day, followed by the afternoon papers, then the evening national news, and finally the late local news.* Once a week, *Time* and *Newsweek* would weigh in with their review of the week that was. This meant that the news took longer to get to us. It also meant that the media didn't have to rush as much. There was considerably more time to do things like check sources, dig up more information, or more carefully consider how to present a story. Today, most reporters simply can't afford to do that. The constant worry about being scooped by a rival news organization means that speed is of the essence. Stories need to be filed more quickly and can't be edited as carefully as they were when the pace was less frenetic. In 2008, the *Washington Post* instituted a "two-touch rule" to speed up their news delivery process—instead of the multiple editorial layers (as many as six in some cases), stories would only be examined twice before appearing in print or online.[17]

All of this unquestionably has an effect on the accuracy of the news. As Bill Kovach, former Washington bureau chief for the *New York Times*, puts it, "Speed, in the news, is the enemy of accuracy. The less time one has to produce something, the more errors it will contain."[18] For example, in their rush to be the first to report the Supreme Court's ruling on the Affordable Care Act, CNN and Fox News pushed out their headlines barely after Chief Justice Roberts read the ruling, erroneously announcing that the law had been ruled unconstitutional. As the *Wall Street Journal* reported the next day, the reports "set off a flurry of confusion among law-makers, candidates, and even the president."[19] Had they waited *literally* two minutes longer, that wouldn't have happened. CNN issued an apology, stat-ing that it regretted "that it didn't wait to report out the full and complete opinion regarding the mandate." Fox, on the other hand, expressed nothing resembling regret, with a spokesperson simply stating that "We gave our viewers the news as it happened."[20] The Poynter Institute's Craig Silverman captured the dynamic well, writing, "Cable news thrives on immediacy; complexity is anathema, especially when it arrives in a moment of

---

*Many people don't even know what an afternoon paper is. That's because almost all of them are gone. And many of the local morning papers don't seem to be far behind, at least in print format.

urgency."[21] The urgency in this case had little to do with the substantive effect of the ruling (most of the law doesn't go into effect until 2014)—it was all about getting the story first.

Most reporters would love to slow down and take time with their stories, but they simply can't because of the constant pressure to churn out more news product, a pressure that has only increased in recent years, with journalists expected to not only write articles but also post to blogs and tweet throughout the day. Because most people actually prefer short stories without a lot of detail, this strategy often works out well from both an economic and consumer-satisfaction standpoint. The result is news that's shorter, snappier, and more entertaining—but ultimately much shallower.

## BIAS 7: PROFIT

All of the previous six biases occur in the service of the profit bias, which is without a doubt the most important of the Seven Deadly Biases as well as an inevitable consequence of a news media operating in a capitalist society. Rule one of capitalism is that you have to make money—or at least break even—to stay in business. For media companies, making money is all about attracting advertisers, who pay most of the bills. American newspapers are almost entirely dependent on ads, which make up 87 percent of their total revenues.[22] To get advertisers, media companies have to attract consumers, and the biases we've looked at are powerful tools for getting people to tune in and keep on coming back.

It's been argued that media companies used to put the public's need to know above considerations of profit. Even if that is true (and it is very much debatable), it's largely immaterial. Back then, less competition meant that media companies didn't have to be as focused on the bottom line. Profit margins of 25 percent or more, made possible by limited competition, also made it possible for media companies to be more civic-minded. Those same profit margins attracted big corporate investors, which led to a wave of media consolidation starting in the late 1990s. These conglomerates tended to be far more focused on the bottom line than previous owners, owing in large part to the demands of investors who were far more interested in share price than news values.

The wave of big media mergers was happening at around the same time as the Internet was becoming a part of everyday life. In the pre-Internet era, news media competition was limited by some extremely high barriers to entry—it took lots of time and money to set up a newspaper or to get a broadcasting license and start a television or radio station. That's the environment that helped create cozy semimonopolies and high profit margins.

But the Internet changed all that because it dramatically lowered barriers to entry in the media market. Worse yet (from the media's perspective) was the creation of services like monster.com and craigslist that destroyed newspapers' classified and help-wanted ad revenues. There was also the issue of charging for online news. The vast majority of the public quickly came to expect online news to be free, and because there was so much competition for the online audience if a company tried to charge for news, consumers could—and did—simply go elsewhere. In the short term, this has been great for us as consumers but awful for news organizations.

In this new, hypercompetitive environment, keeping the share price up meant that costs had to be cut. The care and feeding of reporters isn't cheap, and so many of these cuts came in the form of personnel reductions. This saves some money up front but at a cost: to cover politics with fewer reporters, news organizations can provide diminished coverage, provide more superficial coverage, or try the popular strategy of mixing and matching diminished and superficial coverage. The end result is the same—lower-quality news.

Improving the bottom line has also meant giving the people more of what they want. As we've seen, the Internet allows media companies to get far more detailed information about audience preferences than other forms of media, and it wasn't long before news organizations started putting this information to use. In the newsroom of the *Washington Post*, once considered by many to be the best political newspaper in the country, there are now video screens monitoring the number of hits each article receives, along with red and green lights to indicate whether the site's "traffic goal" for the month is being met. This isn't just a *Washington Post* thing—every news organization pays close attention to the popularity of the stories it posts online. More often than not, the stories that win these minute-by-minute contests aren't in-depth analyses of boring but important political issues. Blame the media if you like, but it's not really their fault—staying in business in this new media world means catering to the desires of the public. You can see this for yourself by checking out the "most read" or "most e-mailed" sections found on just about every major media site.

Media companies aren't in the public service business—they exist to make money for the people who own them. This will be true as long as we have a capitalist economy, and there's little chance of that changing anytime soon. What this means in practical terms is that it's mostly pointless to get upset at all the bias in the media's coverage of politics. As long as it's making money, the media isn't going to change how it covers politics. If you want better political coverage, the change has to come from you.

## NOTES

1. "Press Widely Criticized, but Trusted More Than Other Information Sources," Pew Research Center, September 22, 2011, http://www.people-press.org/2011/09/22/press-widely-criticized-but-trusted-more-than-other-institutions/.

2. "3rd Annual TV News Trust Poll—Public Policy Polling," Public Policy Polling, January 18, 2012, http://www.publicpolicypolling.com/main/2012/01/3rd-annual-tv-news-trust-poll.html.

3. "Tone of News Coverage," Project for Excellence in Journalism, accessed December 21, 2012, http://features.journalism.org/campaign-2012-in-the-media/tone-of-news-coverage/.

4. Tim Groseclose, *Left Turn: How Liberal Media Bias Distorts the American Mind* (New York: St. Martin's Griffin, 2012).

5. Andrew Gelman, "Thoughts on Groseclose Book on Media Bias," The Monkey Cage, July 29, 2011, http://themonkeycage.org/blog/2011/07/29/thoughts-on-groseclose-book-on-media-bias/.

6. "Americans Spending More Time Following the News," Pew Research Center, September 12, 2010, http://www.people-press.org/2010/09/12/americans-spending-more-time-following-the-news/.

7. "Partisan Polarization Surges in Bush, Obama Years," Pew Research Center, June 4, 2012, http://www.people-press.org/2012/06/04/partisan-polarization-surges-in-bush-obama-years/.

8. C. John Sommerville, *How the News Makes Us Dumb* (Downers Grove, IL: InterVarsity Press, 1999), 12.

9. Russell Poldrack, "Multitasking: The Brain Seeks Novelty," Huffington Post, November 17, 2011, http://www.huffingtonpost.com/russell-poldrack/multitasking-the-brain-se_b_334674.html.

10. Steve Benen, "How Health Care Rulings Are Covered," The Washington Monthly, *Political Animal* [blog], June 30, 2011, http://www.washingtonmonthly.com/political-animal/2011_06/how_health_care_rulings_are_co030597.php.

11. Brendan Nyhan, "Scandal Potential: How Political and Media Context Affect the President's Vulnerability to Allegations of Misconduct," working paper, 2012, http://www.dartmouth.edu/~nyhan/scandal-potential.pdf.

12. Brendan Nyhan, "Do Campaign Gaffes Matter? Not to Voters," *Columbia Journalism Review*, June 13, 2012, http://www.cjr.org/swing_states_project/nyhan_gaffes.php.

13. "Public Trust in Government: 1958–2010," Pew Research Center, April 18, 2010, http://people-press.org/trust/.

14. "CNN Poll: Trust in Government at All Time Low," CNN, September 28, 2011, http://politicalticker.blogs.cnn.com/2011/09/28/cnn-poll-trust-in-government-at-all-time-low/.

15. "What Americans Learned from the Media about the Health Care Debate," June 19, 2012, http://www.journalism.org/node/29855.

16. Martin Kaplan, "Welcome to the Infotainment Freak Show," in Andras Szanto, ed., *What Orwell Didn't Know* (New York: Public Affairs, 2007), 140.

17. Jean Yves Chainon, "Editors Weblog—US: WaPo's 21st Century Story Path—Less Hands, Online Deadlines," World Association of Newspapers and News Publishers, March 18, 2008, http://www.editorsweblog.org/2008/03/18/us-wapos-21st-century-story-path-less-hands-online-deadlines.

18. Bill Kovach and Tom Rosenstiel, *Blur: How to Know What's True in the Age of Information Overload* (New York: Reprint, Bloomsbury USA, 2011).

19. Carol E. Lee and Daniel Lippman, "In Moments after Decision, Confusion," *Wall Street Journal*, June 29, 2012, http://online.wsj.com/article/SB10001424052702303649504577495170204412562.html.

20. Andrew Beaujon, "CNN Issues Correction, Fox Issues Statement on Supreme Court Reporting Mistakes," Poynter, June 28, 2012, http://www.poynter.org/latest-news/mediawire/179245/cnn-issues-correction-fox-issue-statement-on-supreme-court-reporting-mistakes/.

21. Craig Silverman, "CNN, Fox News Errors a Series of Real-time Collisions," Poynter, June 29, 2012, http://www.poynter.org/latest-news/regret-the-error/179426/cnn-fox-news-errors-a-series-of-real-time-collisions/.

22. "Daily Newspaper Revenue," *The Economist*, June 17, 2010, http://www.economist.com/node/16380005.

# FIVE

## Irrationality

*The first principle is that you must not fool yourself—and you are the easiest person to fool.*

—Richard Feynman

### IRRATIONALITY AND IGNORANCE

When it comes to politics, there's little question that most Americans are pretty ignorant. A lot of people—presumably people who aren't so ignorant—can get very worked up about this. Some of them even write books with titles like *Just How Stupid Are We?* and *The Dumbest Generation*.[1] Study after study finds that more or less any way you care to measure it, a lot of Americans know very little about politics. It's generally thought (or at least hoped) that political ignorance is correctable through education, which is why most of the people who write books about the sorry state of Americans' political knowledge usually end by calling for some sort of entirely unrealistic plan for reforming political education in the United States.

What all this fails to take into account is irrationality. Irrationality is a much tougher problem than ignorance because most of us have no idea how irrational we can be (and we can be *really* irrational). Philosopher Michael Huemer gets to the heart of the problem in noting that "political irrationality is the greatest problem humanity faces . . . because it *prevents us from solving other problems.*"[2] It can be tough to deal with an irrational person, something most of us know from personal experience. Because finding ways to come to agreement with others is essential to democratic government, irrationality is a huge problem in politics.

Unfortunately, one of the most common types of irrationality is our assumption that we know much more than we actually do. Being ignorant is bad, but believing you're not ignorant when you actually are is a lot worse. If you know you don't know much about the Democratic and Republican presidential candidates you'll probably decide either to not vote or to educate yourself before voting. But if you irrationally overestimate your knowledge, you won't see any need to further educate yourself, and your vote will be less well informed. Pile up enough uninformed votes and you've got a potentially serious problem.

We've all run across people who think they know considerably more than they do, but almost none of us believe that we could possibly be one of those people. Yet there are a multitude of studies demonstrating that we are absolutely horrible self-evaluators who have far more confidence in the rightness of our views than is merited. As neuroscientist Robert Burton says, "Despite how certainty feels, it is neither a conscious choice nor even a thought process. Certainty and similar states of 'knowing what we know' arise out of involuntary brain mechanisms that, like love or anger, function independently of reason."[3]

But if you're like most people, you can look at these studies all day long and never think that *you* might actually be holding on to any irrational political beliefs. You probably feel that your political views are based on facts and that you would be willing to change your views if the facts dictated you do so. There's a good chance you're wrong about this. First, as we will see throughout this chapter, political irrationality comes in many forms and is extremely widespread. Being irrational is part of being human. Nobel Prize–winning psychologist Daniel Kahneman believes that our irrational and rational selves are essentially two different systems. Our nonrational "System 1" is intuitive, fast, always on, and largely unconscious. "System 2"—our rational self—is nonintuitive, calculating, slow, and has to be manually turned on. We'd like to believe that System 2 is in control, but it's not: it's the nonrational System 1 that runs the show.

According to New York University psychologist Jonathan Haidt, our rational self is like a person riding on the elephant that is our irrational self. We can learn to understand our elephant and even train it to some extent, but if the elephant decides it wants to go somewhere, about all we can do is hang on for the ride. The rider might claim to have wanted to go there anyway, but more often than not that's a story our rider tells so it can feel it's in charge. And so it's not really a question of whether or not you're politically irrational. You *are* politically irrational. So am I. So is everyone you know. The real question is *how* irrational we are and what forms our irrationality takes.

Even if you accept that you're holding some questionable political beliefs, there's no guarantee that exposure to the truth will change your views. Political scientists Brendan Nyhan and Jason Reifler studied people's willingness to change their political misperceptions by having them read fake news articles with misleading claims, followed by a correction explaining the errors. (The claims were that the United States found weapons of mass destruction after invading Iraq, that tax cuts increase government revenue, and that President Bush banned stem cell research.) They found that in many cases, corrections had no effect—people kept on believing what they already believed in spite of reputable evidence to the contrary. In some cases the corrections made things worse by actually strengthening incorrect political views—what Nyhan and Reifler call a backfire effect.[4] You might think that smart people are less likely to be irrational, but research on irrationality and intelligence suggests that this may not be the case. In a recent study, psychologists Richard West, Russell Meserve, and Keith Stanovich found that irrational "blind spots" aren't any smaller in smart people and suggest that this is because no matter how smart your rider (System 2) is, your elephant (System 1) is a whole lot bigger, stronger, and faster.[5]

About 2,500 years ago, the oracle at Delphi supposedly pronounced the philosopher Socrates the wisest man in the land. This is said to have puzzled Socrates because he didn't believe he had definitive answers to any truly important questions. In order to see if the oracle was right, Socrates went around ancient Athens talking to people generally considered to be wise to see if he actually knew more than they did. After doing this for a while, Socrates concluded that while he didn't know much, neither did anybody else. What made Socrates wiser than all of the supposedly wise men of his time was his willingness to admit his ignorance.

You're no Socrates (neither am I, obviously). But we can at least aspire to his wisdom by considering the possibility that some of our views about politics are founded on irrationality. Being politically rational is tough, and while perfect political rationality is not in the cards for any of us, we *can* become less irrational. The first step to doing so is accepting our inherent irrationality. After that, it's important to understand the ways we're most likely to be irrational about politics so that we can be in a better position to know when irrationality is most likely to strike.

There are many forms of political irrationality, and taking a close look at all of them would make for a long and boring slog. (More importantly, people tend to forget long lists of things, and it's hard to be on the alert for something you can't remember.) But while the varieties of irrationality are nearly limitless, most political irrationality comes in a few basic forms, all of which are worth examining.

## LOOKISM

Lookism is a stupid word for an important thing: our tendency to judge people based on their physical appearance. Many researchers suggest that this is innate in humans, as a number of studies have found that even infants demonstrate a preference for attractive features.[6] Because of this, we tend to be negatively disposed to people who we find unattractive or weird looking. Glance through pictures of successful politicians and you'll notice most of them have a certain "competent and capable" look. Politicians who don't look like this—especially those who appear particularly youthful or baby-faced—are very much the exception. People seem to naturally gravitate toward strong, authoritative-looking people and away from those who appear weak, nervous, or otherwise unfit, whether they realize it or not.

Television, with its fundamental emphasis on visuals, does more than any other medium to encourage lookism. The 1960 presidential debate—which was not only the first televised presidential debate but the first ever debate between candidates in a presidential general election*—demonstrated very early on how important it was for a politician to look good on TV. Richard Nixon, the Republican nominee, came to the debate looking pale and sickly, the result of an extended stay in the hospital for treatment of a serious knee injury. Further hurting his cause, Nixon refused makeup for the debate, which highlighted his five o'clock shadow (something that showed up really well on the black-and-white television image). John Kennedy, who appeared youthful, vigorous, and confident, was a stark contrast to his opponent.[†] In polls taken after the debate, those who had watched it on TV felt that Kennedy had won, while people who had only heard the debate on the radio concluded that Nixon was the winner.

While over time politicians have gotten a lot smarter about television, there's only so much a clean shave and good makeup can do for a

---

*Many people mistakenly believe that the famous Lincoln-Douglas debates of 1858 were presidential debates when, in fact, Lincoln and Douglas were contending not for the presidency but for an Illinois Senate seat.

†Ironically, it was later revealed that Kennedy suffered from a variety of extremely serious health problems throughout his life—problems he went to great lengths to conceal from the public.

candidate. Many journalists covering the 2008 presidential election commented on how John McCain appeared old and creaky compared to the much younger and more energetic Barack Obama, a contrast that was particularly clear when they shared the stage for presidential debates. More recently, when New Jersey governor Chris Christie was considering a run for the Republican presidential nomination, his weight was a major issue of discussion and, on many occasions, derision. (Christie, who is 5 feet 11 inches, weighed somewhere in excess of 300 pounds at the time.) As Neil Postman observed back in the 1980s, "we may have reached a point where cosmetics has replaced ideology as the field of expertise over which a politician must have competent control."[7] Since then, our culture has become, if anything, even more visually oriented and prone to lookism. It's probably not a coincidence that of the 43 men who have been president of the United States, only four were shorter than the height of the average male at the time, with the last of them—5-foot 7-inch William McKinley—having been elected more than a century ago.

A growing body of academic research has uncovered a strong connection between physical appearance and electability. In a 2005 study done by researchers at Princeton, subjects were shown pictures of the winner and runner up in the 2004 congressional elections and asked to pick the candidate they thought looked more competent. (To ensure that their preconceived notions about the candidates wouldn't affect their judgments, the researchers screened out results when either of the candidates was recognized.) If the appearance of competence didn't matter, the more competent-looking candidate should have been the winner about half of the time. What the researchers found was that nearly 70 percent of the candidates seen as more competent-looking won their elections.[8] Similar studies in 2009[9] and 2010[10] found much the same: the candidate who looked more competent was the winner over 70 percent of the time, a far higher percentage than chance alone would dictate.

The political benefit of looking good seems to extend beyond the ballot box. Researchers at Israel's University of Haifa ranked the attractiveness of every member of the 110th Congress by showing each member's official photograph to 463 Israeli college students (who would be unlikely to recognize any of the people they were ranking). They then compared these attractiveness rankings to the amount of media coverage the members of Congress received. They found that there was a significant relationship between media coverage and attractiveness, with attractiveness being more important to the amount of media coverage than gender, bills sponsored, or even time in office. Importantly, this effect applied *only* to television—attractiveness didn't matter in radio and print coverage. [11]

It's the same with the people who give us our news on TV. We call them journalists or reporters, but it might be more appropriate to use the British term: newsreaders. Having a solid journalism background is unquestionably useful, but if you don't have a certain look you can forget about anchoring the nightly news.* And whether you get your news from a network, Comedy Central, or anywhere in between, it's probably a mature white guy who's anchoring the broadcast. Some claim this demonstrates sexism or racism, but regardless of how you feel about that argument, it's hard to not conclude that there's something about mature white males that a lot of viewers seem to trust, though there's no rational reason for the preference.

Even people who you might think wouldn't be fooled by appearances are affected by lookism. In a well-known experiment conducted in the 1970s, researchers hired a distinguished-looking actor to give medical professionals an energetic but entirely nonsensical lecture on "Mathematical Game Theory as Applied to Physician Education." After the lecture, members of the audience completed a questionnaire rating the quality of the presentation given by "Dr. Fox." The response was overwhelmingly positive, even though the message was specifically designed to make no sense at all.[12] This "Dr. Fox Effect" is evidence that an education is no guarantee of protection from appearance-based irrationality.

We are regularly bombarded with images of politicians, with the onslaught becoming particularly heavy before elections. Those images are carefully crafted to appeal to our lookism, and not just in a positive sense. If you examine images of candidates used by their opponents, you'll see that they almost always make the person look weak, shifty, and untrustworthy. Often, it's something in the eyes that makes us wonder if maybe this person is a bit unhinged. Pair this with some scary, dissonant music, and you can make even the most photogenic candidate seem like a potential menace. We may say that we base our vote on what the candidates say and do, but the evidence suggests that, like it or not, we're also affected by how they look.

## GROUPISM

Being human means being in groups. We're automatically members of certain groups such as our family, nation, race, ethnicity, and generation.

---

*Of the three network news anchors, only CBS's Scott Pelley has a degree in journalism. NBC's Brian Williams dropped out of college, and ABC news anchor Diane Sawyer received her degree in English.

Other group affiliations, such as ideology and political party, we take up later in life, often because other "people like us" are also members. Being part of a group—what psychologists call ingroup affiliation—generally feels good, which makes a lot of sense as early humans who were able to form tight, cohesive groups were a lot more likely to survive and pass on their genes than were rugged individualists (who probably ended up as something's dinner).

But for every *us* there's a *them*. The flip side of favoring people in *our* groups is looking with suspicion on people not in our groups. As a result, we tend to be far less critical of things coming from our group and far more critical of whatever the other group is saying and doing. In a series of studies, Yale psychologist Geoffrey Cohen presented groups of liberals and conservatives with the exact same policy—at times saying it was approved by the Republican Party and at times claiming it was approved by the Democrats. He found that people were more likely to be for the policy when told it came from their party and less likely to be for it when told it came from the other party. This was happening unconsciously because when Cohen asked if the party label was influencing their view of the policy, he was routinely told that it was not a factor—people truly believed they were deciding based on the facts. [13]

Groupism also helps to explain why so many people see the media as ideologically biased against their views, a phenomenon known as the hostile media effect. Scott Reid, a professor of communication at the University of California—Santa Barbara, has studied the hostile media effect by giving Democrats and Republicans neutrally worded polling report articles on candidates, with the only difference being the affiliation of the article's author. When the author was identified as representing a Democratic think tank, Republicans were more likely to rate the article as biased against Republicans. Similarly, telling Democrats that the author was associated with a Republican think tank resulted in their seeing bias against Democrats. [14] Reid's experiments confirm what Cohen and many others have found—we look with suspicion at those whose politics differ from ours—but go even further, providing evidence that we have a tendency to think that people in other groups are actively out to get us.

This doesn't just apply to complex policies or interpretation of polling reports. We even seem to inhabit different factual realities based on our political party. In a 2012 YouGov survey, people were asked a very straightforward question: "Do you think the unemployment rate has increased or decreased since Barack Obama became president?" Eighty-two percent of the Republicans surveyed said that unemployment had increased, with 62 percent saying it had increased a lot. Democrats had a very different view—only 27 percent believed that unemployment had increased at all, and 59 percent thought it had actually gone down. Amazingly, 9 percent of Democrats surveyed actually believed that unemployment had decreased a lot since President Obama took office.[15] What's important here isn't who is right on this particular issue (at the time of the survey, unemployment had increased half a percentage point from the month of Obama's inauguration). The important thing is that the Republican and Democrat groups had two very different views of reality.

This applies to how we see candidates as well: a recent study on views of 2008 presidential candidates Barack Obama and John McCain found that people asked about their race (thereby reminding them of their racial group status) were more likely to believe slurs about the candidate who was not of the same race. There was a similar effect with age—the group that was asked to list their age (they were all young college students) was significantly more likely to believe that John McCain was senile than those not given the age-group prompt.[16]

Election results demonstrate the powerful pull of groupism. In the 2012 presidential election, 92 percent of Democrats and 93 percent of Republicans voted for "their guy." Race and religion also had a powerful pull: 93 percent of black voters cast their votes for Obama, with Romney getting 78 percent of the Mormon vote.[17] These entirely commonplace results might be the most compelling example of the pull that our group ties exert on our political choices.

## STORIES OVER NUMBERS

People like stories—math and numbers and statistics not so much. Partly, this is because we use language all the time, and so it's easier for us to grasp stories (at least simple stories) than it is to understand numerical data. But it's also because numbers, by themselves, generally lack the emotional content that draws us in and helps us to remember. Our preference for stories is why both politicians and the media covering them think in terms of crafting a narrative far more often than they consider analyzing the data (at least for public consumption). As *The American Prospect*'s Paul Waldman puts it, "All successful candidates have had a coherent, appealing story, while the losers tell bad stories—or, more often, no story at all."[18]

This doesn't mean we don't care about number-centric issues, as recent history demonstrates. The Tea Party movement was built on budgetary concerns, and Occupy Wall Street focused almost exclusively on the distribution of income—two of the most number-oriented political issues there are. But if you pay attention to how people relate to these issues, you'll see that they mostly do it by telling stories instead of analyzing data. And the stories they tell are usually simple and easy to remember, along the lines of, "Democrats want to give handouts to takers" or "Republicans only care about helping rich people." The most common type of political story we're told involves that old standby, "Good versus Evil"—with "good" representing us and whatever party, issue, or candidate we support, of course.* We've been hearing this story, in various guises, from the time we were children, and so it immediately resonates with us. But it's a story that tends to reinforce a version of reality that's often dangerously simplistic. Behavioral economist Tyler Cowen emphasizes this in his advice to people who are being told this story. "As a simple rule of thumb, just imagine every time you're telling a good vs. evil story, you're basically lowering your IQ by ten points or more."[19] Buying into stories without question may not literally make you dumber, but it's almost certain to close you off to important parts of political reality.

There are often numbers behind the political stories we're told, but very few of us bother to take a good hard look at them. One reason for this is that figuring out whether the numbers support a claim isn't always an easy thing to do. In addition (no pun intended), simply tracking down the numbers can be hard work. Even online, it takes extra effort to find and examine data; if you get your news from a nononline source, which the majority of Americans still do, you need to first write down (or remember) the data source and then go online and search for it. Very few people are going to bother with all that.

What this means is that politicians and pundits can more easily mislead us because they know how difficult it can be to check the numbers. At times, they'll even flat-out lie and get away with it. As political pollster Frank Luntz has observed, "A compelling story, even if factually inaccurate, can be more emotionally compelling than a dry recitation of the truth."[20]

But outright lies are problematic because getting caught in one can lead to a lot of negative publicity. A more common way our distaste for numbers is used against us is through data manipulation. Manipulating data isn't exactly lying—it's more like finding ways of highlighting things that support your viewpoint. And so the worst you can usually say about someone who does it is that they're basing their conclusions on questionable assumptions or using an inappropriate method of analysis. This isn't exactly the sort of stirring denunciation that will grab headlines or make much of an impact on voters.

---

*Which ties directly into groupism. Irrational political beliefs often clump together like that.

Our preference for stories over numbers means that we can often be convinced of something by a string of stories, even if they aren't representative of the whole. In many cases, what both the media and politicians are trying to convince us of is that things are really, really bad. In the last few years, this has been the template for countless news items about mortgage foreclosures: a typical story might begin with something about the awful state of the housing market, with mention of millions of foreclosures and possibly some statistics from particularly hard-hit areas. Then there are quotes from two or three homeowners who are angry or scared because they have either lost or are on the verge of losing their home to foreclosure. (Bonus points if the homeowner has young children.) There will also be a quote or two from a "housing expert" (frequently an economist) about how bad things are and the dim prospects for the future. That's a compelling—if depressing—story, one that millions of people have been told for years. It's not untrue, but it most definitely represents an extremely limited view of what's going on in the housing market.

Another housing story—one that you probably haven't heard—goes like this. Industry data indicates that only 0.5 percent of houses will *ever* be foreclosed on. [21] In 2010, the height of the foreclosure crisis, only 2.23 percent of mortgage holders received a foreclosure notice, and fewer than that ended up losing their homes to foreclosure.[22] In other words, when things were at their very worst, nearly 98 percent of homeowners *weren't* foreclosed on. This isn't to say that foreclosures aren't both awful and a very real problem, but the multiple-anecdote-based format of so many news stories may lead us to overestimate the extent of the problem. Stories can be compelling, but when they're taken out of their larger context—a context numbers can often provide—they can be misleading.

## OVERSIMPLIFICATION

When things happen, especially when they affect us, we generally want to know why they happened. But when what happens is the result of countless people and institutions making a myriad of decisions over an extended period of time, our ability to understand can be overwhelmed, particularly if we don't have the time, ability, or inclination to deeply delve into causes and contributing factors. Dealing with difficult questions leads to what psychologists call cognitive strain, which is something we try very hard to minimize. But although we don't want to strain ourselves, we do want to think we know what's going on, so we rely on a simplified version of reality. Daniel Kahneman has found that if our rational System 2 can't find a quick answer to a complex question, our default response most definitely *isn't* to dig for more information or accept our ignorance. Instead, we quickly (and usually unconsciously) substitute a much simpler question and answer that. So, for instance, instead of trying to answer the question "Who has a better tax reform plan: Mitt Romney or Barack Obama?" many of us will substitute the far simpler question, "Who do I like better: Mitt Romney or Barack Obama?" and use our answer to this question to answer the tax-reform question. This cognitive shortcut gives us the positive feeling of having answered the question, even though we're not answering the question we'd like to believe we're answering.

This is a problem because our simple answers—regardless of whether we come up with them on our own or are fed them by the media (or some combination of the two)—almost always leave out a lot of important stuff. This isn't something we generally hear from our elected officials because they understand that giving us an answer, even one they know is dangerously oversimplified, will generally satisfy us more than being told "It's complicated, but if you have some time and you're willing to be patient with me, I'll try to explain to the best of my understanding what's going on." People who study public policy often don't even use the word *problem* to refer to many complex issues because saying that something is a problem makes it seem like it's a single, definable thing that might also have a single, clearly identifiable cause and solution. In 1973, University of California—Berkeley professors Horst Rittel and Melvin Webber came up with a new way to describe the many incredibly complex issues modern society faces—they called them "wicked problems." The term caught on because it did an excellent job of capturing the confusing, interconnected, constantly shifting nature of politics and public policy.*

Health care policy is a classic wicked problem. It's been an issue of considerable debate in recent years, with President Obama and congressional Democrats enacting major changes to the system in the form of the Affordable Care Act (a.k.a. Obamacare). The issue was hotly debated and received intense media coverage. Positions quickly solidified into slogans, and the public was repeatedly bludgeoned with variations of two basic themes: "coldhearted Republicans don't want poor people to have coverage" and "Democrats want to destroy our free market economy with their socialist plan." Millions of Americans seized on these ridiculously oversimplified explanations as adequate depictions of the policy positions of the opposition.

Health care is a huge part of our economy—in 2010, total health care spending reached $2.6 trillion dollars, or 17.9 percent of the United

---

*Mess* is also frequently used to describe wicked problems (such as "the housing mess" or "the health care mess").

States' gross domestic product.[23] It's an issue that involves all of us, and fully understanding how it works and how various legislative changes might affect the system requires at least a basic knowledge of a number of fields: economic theory, health care economics, medical practice and technology, and decades of legislative history, at the very least. The small percentage of people who are anywhere close to conversant in those areas almost all conclude that the health care system in the United States is really big and enormously complicated, which means that nobody can truly predict everything a major change like the Affordable Care Act will do to health care in the United States. But it's a fair bet that it won't all go according to plan, and there will almost certainly be a bunch of unintended consequences. Some of these consequences might be pretty good, and some might be pretty bad. There's really no way to know. That is an extremely unsatisfying conclusion to come to. It also happens to be as close to the truth as we can get. Of course, almost nobody really wants to hear (or believe) that.

Oversimplification leads us to expect too much from political leaders, particularly the president. While the president is the most powerful political figure in the country, he is only one part of a system designed to force compromise and make major change very difficult. Many people expect a new president to be able to come in and get things done, not realizing that changing anything of real substance in government is a lot like turning around a supertanker, in the middle of a storm, with half the crew trying to steer the other way. No politician is going to get people all worked up with a lecture on the separation of powers, or the legislative process, or how very hard it is to get things done, and so we end up with vastly overblown promises to "change the culture" of Washington, promises that can even come to define a candidate's campaign, as in the 2008 Obama campaign's "Change We Can Believe In" slogan.

The candidates themselves may not believe this (at least not as much as they claim to), but they know it's what people want to hear. The problem comes when the public's unreasonably high expectations, based on an extremely oversimplified understanding of government, are not met. Over time this causes people to lose faith in government because again and again politicians promise them things they can't realistically deliver. We see this with depressing regularity in politics; not too long ago it was expressed very well by Velma Hart, an Obama supporter speaking to the president at a town hall meeting in September 2010:

> Quite frankly, I'm exhausted. Exhausted of defending you, defending your administration, defending the mantle of change that I voted for, and deeply disappointed with where we are right now. I've been told

that I voted for a man who was going to change things in a meaningful way for the middle class. I'm one of those people, sir, and I'm waiting. And I don't feel it yet.[24]

Research by the Pulitzer Prize-winning site PolitiFact gives us a broader view of the endemic promise making and promise breaking in politics. According to PolitiFact, Obama made over 500 promises during his 2008 presidential campaign—a fairly staggering total. As you might expect, that's far too many promises to keep: after a full term in office, President Obama has managed to fully keep only 44 percent of them.[25] President Obama is regularly blasted for his broken promises by Republicans, but overpromising is one of the few things in Washington that's fully bipartisan. Everybody does it because we'd all like to believe that our problems, and their solutions, are relatively simple. In politics that's almost never the case.

## CONFIRMATION BIAS

Confirmation bias is our tendency to look for evidence that supports what we already believe and try really hard to ignore anything that might prove us wrong. This is the most important way in which we are politically irrational, and it's also the toughest to deal with. This is because we *love* feeling right—almost as much as we hate feeling wrong. As a result, we're willing to work really hard to find the facts and arguments that best fit our beliefs. By the same token, we generally don't go out of our way to prove ourselves wrong. As Winston Churchill put it, "Men occasionally stumble over the truth, but most of them pick themselves up and hurry off as if nothing had happened."

Confirmation bias means more than simply giving the benefit of the doubt to our own beliefs. It involves something psychologists call "motivated reasoning," a process in which we regularly and systematically overestimate the evidence and arguments in favor of our views and underestimate or discredit inconvenient truths. Psychologist Jonathan Haidt likens our reasoning ability to a press secretary for our emotions. The press secretary's job isn't to weigh the facts and make decisions but instead to justify whatever decisions have already been made. There are a seemingly endless number of studies that have found confirmation bias affecting people's views on everything from sex[26] to how students evaluate their professors[27], to political beliefs.[28]

An analysis of a May 2012 poll from YouGov by Princeton political scientist Larry Bartels is a case in point. In the poll, people were asked whether "The Supreme Court should be able to throw out any law it considers unconstitutional"—a power that has been well established for over 200 years. The question was asked just before the Supreme Court ruled on the constitutionality of the biggest legislative endeavor of the Obama presidency—the health care reform law. Bartels found that over half of the people who wanted the law to stand believed that the Court didn't have the power to overturn unconstitutional laws, a power the Court unquestionably does have. By comparison, nearly 80 percent of the law's opponents believed that the Supreme Court could throw out unconstitutional laws.[29]

Our need to be right stems in large part from our discomfort with something called cognitive dissonance, which social psychologists Carol Tavris and Elliot Aronson explain as "a state of tension that occurs whenever a person holds two cognitions (ideas, attitudes, beliefs, opinions) that are psychologically inconsistent."[30] The more evidence we see that contradicts our beliefs, the greater the tension. The rational way to resolve this tension is to revise our beliefs in light of new evidence, but that's extremely difficult for most people. In some areas of life, we will make a real effort to do this, but when it comes to politics it's not worth the trouble for most of us.

This is in large part due to the nature of democratic government in a big country. At some level, we understand that while every vote counts, our individual vote counts for very little—in a presidential election, you've got about a 1 in 60 million chance of casting the decisive vote.[31] Even in the small minority of elections where candidates have almost equal support, your vote is extraordinarily unlikely to tilt the scales. Considering how emotionally taxing and time consuming it can be to critically examine our beliefs, for most of us it makes more sense to not bother because we know in the back of our minds that even if we are wrong (not that we are, of course), it's not really that big of a deal. As political scientist Anthony Downs has observed, "It is irrational to be politically well-informed because the low returns from data simply do not justify their cost in time and other resources."[32] In other words, holding irrational beliefs can actually be the *rational* course of action, from an individual cost-benefit perspective. The only sort of benefits politicians can offer most voters are indirect and in the future: "Vote for me and I'll cut your taxes, fix the economy, reduce unemployment, etc., etc." The idea that "maybe, on the extremely slim chance my truly informed vote matters, the person I choose might be able to do some of the things he's promised, which could potentially be to my benefit" isn't much of an incentive to study up. Keeping old, irrational beliefs also makes good sense physiologically because serious thinking is literally hard work—work that measurably lowers the body's blood glucose levels. Humans naturally seek to conserve energy, and so we avoid straining our minds without good reason. It's no wonder why getting people to take a serious look at their political beliefs is so difficult.

Confirmation bias predisposes us to selective exposure, which is our tendency to consume political media with which we agree and avoid media we disagree with. Selective exposure is why so many Republicans watch Fox News, and why the *Huffington Post* is a favorite website of Democrats. As we've already seen, thanks to the Internet it's easier than ever to build your very own personalized political selective-exposure machine, something that's guaranteed to give you regular confirmation of whatever you might happen to believe (no matter how unmoored from reality your political beliefs may be).

Confirmation bias doesn't make us shut out *all* information that contradicts our beliefs. In fact, many people will tell you that their favorite political pundit—whether it's Bill O'Reilly, Glenn Beck, Jon Stewart, or whomever—makes a real effort to present both sides. It's just that the other side is obviously stupid or wrong (or both). That's probably because the evidence that's being presented for the other side is what psychologists call weakly dissonant, meaning that it's presented in a way that magnifies its shortcomings. We really like weak dissonance because it allows us to pretend that we're fairly considering an opposing argument when what we're really doing is using a shallow, unfair version of that argument to make us feel better about our own view. One of our favorite ways of doing this is by focusing on out-of-context quotes from politicians that make them look stupid or corrupt (or both).

Even when we see the exact same thing as someone with differing views, we often interpret it differently. This is what's known as selective perception, an excellent explanation of which is provided by Farhad Manjoo in his book *True Enough*:

> Selective perception says that even when two people of opposing ideologies overcome their tendency toward selective exposure and choose to watch the same thing, they may still end up being pushed apart from each other. That's because they really won't be experiencing the same thing—whether it's a football game, a presidential assassination, or a terrorist attack, each of them will have seen, or, felt, and understood thing vastly differently from the others who have experienced it."[33]

One of the main reasons we perceive things differently from those with different views is that when we evaluate ourselves or "our side" we usually consider context and mitigating circumstances. a favor we don't extend to the views of those we're not positively disposed toward. This tendency, which psychologists call fundamental attribution error, pops up all the time in politics. For example, you may have heard about Romney having strapped his family's dog Seamus on the roof of their car on a family vacation trip. "Animal cruelty!" shouted Democrats, many of whom argued that this demonstrated a fundamental character flaw that made Romney entirely unfit for the presidency. But Romney supporters were more likely to see the story differently, pointing out that Seamus was in a carrier secured to the vehicle's roof rack and that Romney had even designed a shield so that Seamus would be protected from the wind. Mitt Romney isn't cruel to animals, goes this version of reality. In fact, he's the sort of guy who cares so much about animals that he takes the family pet on vacation instead of abandoning it to a cold, impersonal kennel. And even those Romney supporters who think dogs shouldn't be put on the top of station wagons don't see the incident as an indictment of Romney's character. They view it as a small error in judgment committed under trying circumstances (a 12-hour car ride with five kids surely qualifies) over a quarter century ago—the same facts but very different interpretations, thanks to the fundamental attribution error.

We see selective perception at work all the time in public opinion polls. A result from a September 2010 American Research Group poll is typical: 27 percent of those surveyed said they believed the economy was getting better, but among people who disapproved of President Obama, only 5 percent believed things were improving. This is in stark contrast to the views of those who had a positive view of President Obama—61 percent of them felt that the economy was getting better.[34] It's the same economy, but supporters and detractors of President Obama saw it in very different terms. This pattern holds for just about every political issue you can think of. For instance, research by Dan Kahan, Hank Jenkins-Smith, and Donald Braman has found that conservatives consistently underestimate the threat posed by global climate change, whereas liberals consistently overestimate the threat posed by nuclear waste.[35] In each case, there's little question that people's preexisting political views have a significant effect on their evaluations of reality.

What this means is that simply getting more information about an issue won't change our minds if we're unaware of our tendency toward selective exposure and perception. As political scientists Brendan Nyhan and Jason Reifler have demonstrated, exposing people to accurate information generally doesn't change their views and may sometimes even backfire by actually strengthening inaccurate views. The more information we selectively gather and perceive, the more entrenched our views are likely to become and the harder they'll be to change. This often results in what's known of as naïve realism—the heartfelt belief that our view is the only reasonable one and that if someone believes otherwise, they must be ignorant (unaware of all the facts), stupid (unable to properly understand those facts), or just plain bad (bad). There are plenty of ignorant, stupid, and bad people in the world. But because of our naïve realism, we almost certainly overestimate how many there actually are. And we almost never consider the possibility that *we* might be one of those ignorant, stupid, or bad people.

If you set out to become completely rational when it comes to politics, you're going to fail. Irrationality is a big part of who we are, and no matter how hard you try, you'll regularly fall into lookism and groupism, favor stories over numbers, oversimplify political reality, and make an extra effort to prove that you're right. That's true whether you're a political novice or president of the United States. But while perfect political rationality is out of reach, we can become a little less irrational if we keep in mind all the ways we err in trying to make sense of the political world.

## NOTES

1. Rick Shenkman, *Just How Stupid Are We?: Facing the Truth about the American Voter* (New York: Reprint, Basic Books, 2009); Mark Bauerlein, *The Dumbest Generation: How the Digital Age Stupefies Young Americans and Jeopardizes Our Future* (New York: Tarcher, 2009).

2. Michael Huemer, "Why People Are Irrational about Politics," accessed December 21, 2012, http://home.sprynet.com/~owl1/irrationality.htm.

3. Robert Burton, *On Being Certain* (New York: St. Martin's, 2009), xi.

4. Brendan Nyhan and Jason Reifler, "When Corrections Fail: The Persistence of Political Misperceptions," *Political Behavior* 32, no. 2 (March 30, 2010): 303–330.

5. Richard F. West, Russell J. Meserve, and Keith E. Stanovich, "Cognitive Sophistication Does Not Attenuate the Bias Blind Spot," *Journal of Personality and Social Psychology* (June 4, 2012), http://www.ncbi.nlm.nih.gov/pubmed/22663351.

6. Jennifer L. Ramsey et al., "Origins of a Stereotype: Categorization of Facial Attractiveness by 6-Month-Old Infants," *Developmental Science* 7, no. 2 (2004): 201–211.

7. Neil Postman, *Amusing Ourselves to Death: Public Discourse in the Age of Show Business*, 20th Anniversary Edition (New York: Penguin [Non-Classics], 2005), 4.

8. A. Todorov, A. N. Mandisodza, A. Goren, and C. C. Hall, "Inferences of Competence from Faces Predict Election Outcomes," *Science* 308 (2005): 1623–1626.

9. J. Antonakis and O. Dalgas, "Predicting Elections: Child's Play!" *Science* 323 (2009): 1183.

10. Chappell Lawson et al., "Looking Like a Winner: Candidate Appearance and Electoral Success in New Democracies," *World Politics* 62, no. 04 (2010): 561–593.

11. Israel Waismel-Manor and Yariv Tsfati, "Why Do Better-Looking Members of Congress Receive More Television Coverage?" *Political Communication* 28, no. 4 (2011): 440.

12. D. J. Merritt, "Bias, the Brain, and Student Evaluations of Teaching," *St. John's Law Review* 82, no. 1 (2008): 235–287.

13. Geoffrey L. Cohen, "Party over Policy: The Dominating Impact of Group Influence on Political Beliefs," *Journal of Personality and Social Psychology* 85, no. 5 (November 2003): 808–822.

14. Scott A. Reid, "A Self-Categorization Explanation for the Hostile Media Effect," *Journal of Communication* 62, no. 3 (2012): 381–399.

15. Larry Bartels, "Our Own Facts," YouGov, March 12, 2012, http://today.yougov.com/news/2012/03/12/our-own-facts/.

16. Spee Kosloff et al., "Smearing the Opposition: Implicit and Explicit Stigmatization of the 2008 U.S. Presidential Candidates and the Current U.S. President," *Journal of Experimental Psychology* 139 (2010): 383–398.

17. "2012 Fox News Exit Polls," Fox News, accessed December 21, 2012, http://www.foxnews.com/politics/elections/2012-exit-poll.

18. Paul Waldman, "The Power of the Campaign Narrative," *The American Prospect*, July 17, 2007, http://prospect.org/article/power-campaign-narrative.

19. Tyler Cowen, transcript from TEDxMidAtlantic talk, November 5, 2009, accessed December 21, 2012, http://lesswrong.com/r/discussion/lw/8w1/transcript_tyler_cowen_on_stories.

20. Oliver Burkeman, "Memo Exposes Bush's New Green Strategy," *The Guardian*, March 4, 2003, http://www.guardian.co.uk/environment/2003/mar/04/usnews.climatechange.

21. "NeighborWorks America Foreclosure Statistics," FDIC.gov, accessed December 21, 2012, http://www.fdic.gov/about/comein/files/foreclosure_statistics.pdf.

22. "2010 Year-End U.S. Metro Foreclosure Report," RealityTrac, January 26, 2011, http://www.realtytrac.com/content/press-releases/2010-year-end-us-metro-foreclosure-report-6317.

23. "Historical National Health Care Expenditures," Centers for Medicare & Medicaid Services, April 11, 2012, http://www.cms.gov/Research-Statistics-Data-and-Systems/Statistics-Trends-and-Reports/NationalHealthExpendData/NationalHealthAccountsHistorical.html.

24. Tunku Varadarajan, "Velma Hart: Obama Supporter Taken in by Her Own Illusions," The Daily Beast, September 21, 2010, http://www.thedailybeast.com/blogs-and-stories/2010-09-21/velma-hart-obama-supporter-taken-in-by-her-own-illusions/.

25. "The Obameter: Tracking Obama's Campaign Promises," PolitiFact, accessed December 19, 2012, http://www.politifact.com/truth-o-meter/promises/obameter/.

26. Michael Marks and R. Fraley, "Confirmation Bias and the Sexual Double Standard," *Sex Roles* 54, no. 1 (2006): 19–26.

27. April Kelly-Woessner and Matthew C. Woessner, "My Professor Is a Partisan Hack: How Perceptions of a Professor's Political Views Affect Student Course Evaluations," *PS: Political Science and Politics* 39, no. 3 (July 1, 2006): 495–501.

28. Charles S. Taber and Milton Lodge, "Motivated Skepticism in the Evaluation of Political Beliefs," *American Journal of Political Science* 50, no. 3 (July 1, 2006): 755–769.

29. Larry Bartels, "Democratic Principles Are Sometimes Inconvenient," YouGov, May 19, 2012, http://today.yougov.com/news/2012/05/19/democratic-principles-are-sometimes-inconvenient/.

30. Carol Tavris and Elliot Aronson, *Mistakes Were Made (But Not by Me): Why We Justify Foolish Beliefs, Bad Decisions, and Hurtful Acts* (Orlando, FL: Reprint, Mariner Books, 2008), 13.

31. Andrew Gelman, Nate Silver, and Aaron Edlin, "What Is the Probability Your Vote Will Make a Difference?" *Economic Inquiry* 50, no. 2 (2012): 321–326.

32. Anthony Downs, *An Economic Theory of Democracy* (New York: Addison Wesley, 1997), 94.

33. Farhad Manjoo, *True Enough: Learning to Live in a Post-Fact Society* (Hoboken, NJ: John Wiley & Sons, 2009), 71.

34. "Obama Job Approvals and the National Economy," American Research Group, December 21, 2012, http://americanresearchgroup.com/economy/.

35. Dan M. Kahan, Hank Jenkins-Smith, and Donald Braman, "Cultural Cognition of Scientific Consensus," *Journal of Risk Research* 14, no. 1 (2010): 1.

# SIX

## Bad Arguments

### POLITICAL NEWS AND POLITICAL ARGUMENTS

Successful politicians, regardless of their party or ideology, all share one thing in common—they're able to get a majority of voters to buy three basic arguments. These three basic arguments are (1) here's why you should vote for me (and be very concerned by, and maybe even a little afraid of, my opponent); (2) here's why you should support my excellent policy (and oppose the other side's awful alternatives), and (3) here's why I deserve the credit when things go right (and why my opponents deserve the blame when things go wrong).

It would be nice to think that the most reasonable arguments win out in the end, but if you've read this far you know this isn't going to be a chapter about how the most reasonable arguments win out in the end. Sometimes the winning argument (meaning the argument that a majority of the voters accept) *is* actually the most reasonable one, but there's no question that many of the political arguments that prevail in the real world are deeply flawed. You don't have to be a rocket scientist (or even a political scientist) to realize that it's not good to base political decisions affecting the lives of millions of people on bad arguments.

There are a number of reasons why people make bad arguments. One is that making a good political argument is often difficult because politics almost always involves complex issues that don't lend themselves to simple arguments. Another reason is that many people don't have the patience to absorb thorough, well-developed arguments. If your job depends on getting people to buy those three basic political arguments, you can't say, "Well, the public isn't interested in good arguments, so I'll just give up," at least not if you want to keep working in politics. Instead, you find a way to convince people without using complex arguments. And as we'll see, many simple but logically flawed arguments can be very convincing.

If you want to make smart political choices, you need to be able to spot bad arguments. To do this, you first have to understand how good arguments work. Both good and bad arguments have a conclusion, which is the thing that you're being asked to accept. What makes good arguments good is that they give you compelling and logical reasons to accept the conclusion.* The thing that makes bad arguments so tricky is that many of them *appear* to give compelling and logical reasons for accepting the conclusion.

These seemingly compelling and logical reasons are called *fallacies*. There are at least 100 different fallacies, a review of which would be tedious to the point of cruelty.† Thankfully, you only need to be familiar with the dozen or so that routinely pop up in political arguments. In the rest of the chapter, we'll take a look at these fallacies.

## APPEAL TO EMOTION

The appeal to emotion is a good place to start because it's both extremely common and very easy to understand. It happens whenever someone bases their argument on how you feel, instead of what you think. Because emotions—particularly anger and fear—are really powerful, can be activated quickly, and often short-circuit reason, the appeal to emotion is part of many political arguments. But it usually doesn't appear in its pure form because raw appeals to emotion are generally unconvincing without some structure, however flimsy, to support them. The appeal to Emotion is sort of the condiment of political arguments—it's not a stand-alone dish, but it can do wonders for spicing up an otherwise humdrum argument or masking the rank odor of an argument that would be otherwise unpalatable.

It's difficult to go anywhere and not be hit with appeals to emotion. You can hear it loud and clear when Rush Limbaugh tells his 15 million listeners,

---

*In the language of formal logic these reasons are called *premises*. In a sound argument (*sound* is the formal logic term for what I'm calling a good argument), accepting the premises means that you must also accept the conclusion.
†If you'd like a big list of logical fallacies, yourlogicalfallacyis.com has information on over two dozen of them.

"I think it can now be said, without equivocation—without equivocation—that this man hates this country. He is trying—Barack Obama is trying—to dismantle, brick by brick, the American dream."[1] It's there too in the snarky headline in the popular liberal blog *The Daily Kos*, which asks, "Can Romney Interact with ANYONE without Insulting Them?"[2] It's not just the media—political campaigns are happy to pile on. From April to July of 2012, the Romney campaign ran over *50,000* negative campaign ads brimming with appeals to emotion. That sounds like a lot, but it's nothing compared to the Obama campaign, which more than doubled that total.[3] If you were watching TV in the summer of 2012, there's a good chance that you saw many of these appeals to emotion, like the Obama ad with Mitt Romney croaking out "America the Beautiful" while headlines about Romney's "Swiss bank accounts" and offshore "tax havens" went by,[4] or the Romney ad on the "Obama stimulus money" showing piles of burning currency falling to the ground (accompanied by ominous music, of course).[5]

Fear is one of the most appealed-to emotions in political arguments, with anger running a close second. That's because negative emotions are often more memorable than positive ones, according to political scientists Richard Lau, Lee Sigelman, and Ivy Brown Rovner, who examined the findings of over 100 studies on negative campaigning.[6] Surprisingly, they found that even though negative campaign ads are more memorable, they don't seem to be more effective. The reasons for this aren't entirely clear, though one possibility is that negative ads make people think less of both the person being attacked and the person doing the attacking. One effect that negative ads *do* seem to have, according to Lau and his coauthors, is "lower trust in government, a lessened sense of political efficacy, and possibly a darker public mood," which they suggest is due not just to the negative ads themselves but also to media coverage of the negative ads.*

When thinking about the appeal to emotion, it's good to remember the analogy that psychologist Jonathan Haidt makes between reason and emotion: reason is the rider and emotion is the elephant. Whether it's a stirring patriotic message or a brutal takedown of a political opponent, the appeal to emotion is designed to speak directly to the elephant, bypassing the puny rider. That's what makes it one of the most common—and most effective—bad arguments in politics.

---

*You might be wondering why there are so many negative ads if they don't actually work. It could be that the extremely large body of political science research on the effects of negative advertising is wrong. Or maybe politicians and their media consultants are irrational, just like normal people.

## VAGUENESS

In order to accept an argument, you have to know what exactly it is you're accepting. People making political arguments often use terms that don't have clear meanings. Sometimes this is innocent enough—politics is full of squishy concepts that can be tough to define with great precision. But in many cases the people trying to convince you of something are being intentionally vague. Their hope is that if they don't define their terms, you'll unconsciously insert your own preferred definition, making it more likely that you'll buy their overall argument.

"The middle class" is a classic example of this. Obviously, the middle class has to be between the upper and lower classes, but that doesn't help much because there's no set understanding of how big that middle is. Is it the middle third? Why not 50 percent, or even the middle two-thirds? There's no particular reason to choose one "middle" over the others, aside from going with whatever best helps your argument. In surveys, around half of all Americans tend to define themselves as middle class—by this definition, "middle class" would apply just as much to family with an income of $25,000 a year as it would to one making $75,000 a year. Looking at it this way, it seems like a "middle 50%" definition is awfully broad. That doesn't even get into the issue of what a family is these days or the fact that $50,000 for a family of two is a whole lot different than the same $50,000 for a family of four.

That's exactly the point. Politicians know that you'll probably see yourself as part of the middle class, and so they have a very definite interest in being vague. Using the phrase "families making between $25,000 and $75,000 a year" would only serve to emphasize the gap between those two ends of the range. Also, putting it that way is a lot clunkier than simply saying "the middle class."

People who practice politics for a living are generally pretty smart—when they use a vague term, it's a good bet that they're using it in the hope that you don't spend too much time thinking about what it actually means.

## HASTY GENERALIZATION

A person makes a hasty generalization by basing a conclusion, or asking you to accept a conclusion, on insufficient evidence. The reason hasty generalizations can seem legitimate is that they are based on *some* evidence—just not enough of it.

Our political culture, which focuses relentlessly on what's going on this very minute, is a breeding ground for hasty generalizations. Rushing to judgment is a lot more fun, exciting, and lucrative than sitting around waiting for more complete information. Because the focus is so much on the here and now, political commentators know there's little downside to most hasty generalizations. If you're right, you'll look smart, and maybe even prescient. If it turns out you're wrong, it's no big deal because almost nobody will remember what you said in the first place. And so it is entirely rational for people who write or talk about politics to make hasty generalizations. To a certain extent, this is true for politicians as well, though because their past statements are often closely scrutinized, hasty generalizations can come back to haunt them.*

Perhaps the most well-known political hasty generalization in recent memory has to do with the war in Iraq. The Bush administration made a case for invading Iraq largely by arguing that Saddam Hussein's regime possessed weapons of mass destruction (WMDs). A great deal of time and effort was put into convincing Congress, the American public, and the international community that there was enough evidence to support the view that Iraq was in possession of WMDs. Shortly before the invasion began, National Security Advisor Condoleezza Rice essentially admitted that the administration was acting on imperfect intelligence information but argued that "there will always be some uncertainty" and urged people to take the leap and accept the administration's conclusions because "We don't want the smoking gun to be a mushroom cloud."[7] The American public largely accepted this argument: shortly before the invasion began, a Gallup poll found nearly two-thirds of Americans in favor of military action.[8] In the end, no WMDs were found, and subsequent reviews of the administration's case strongly suggested that solid evidence for WMDs was lacking. For better or worse, the Bush administration asked the public to make what turned out to be a hasty generalization, something a sizable majority of that public was convinced to do.

## ARGUMENT BY INNUENDO

When someone commits this fallacy, they are asking you to believe a conclusion based on what they have suggested but not proven. All of the factual information in an argument by innuendo may be accurate—which

---

*Which is why it's a smart political move to combine a hasty generalization with a healthy dose of vagueness. That way, if someone says, for example, "You said that the troop surge in Iraq would be a disaster, but it turned out really well," the politician can respond that by "disaster" he meant that it would do little to contribute to the long-term democratic health of Iraqi society while costing American money and lives.

makes it seem convincing on the surface—but on closer inspection, that information turns out not to fully support the conclusion. Here's a good example of argument by innuendo at work, taken from a 2010 profile of former Fox News personality Glenn Beck:

> President Obama is not a Muslim, Beck has said, correctly. But Beck can't help wondering aloud on his show: "He needlessly throws his hat into the ring to defend the ground-zero mosque. He hosts Ramadan dinners, which a president can do. But then you just add all of this stuff up—his wife goes against the advice of the advisers, jets to Spain for vacation. What does she do there? She hits up the Alhambra palace mosque. Fine, it's a tourist attraction. But is there anything more to this? Are they sending messages? I don't know. I don't know."[9]

It's clear that Beck wants the listener to believe that President Obama may have inappropriate Muslim sympathies. But he never comes out and says this. In fact, he essentially inoculates himself from counterattack by saying that President Obama is not a Muslim and that he "doesn't know" what all the facts he presented mean. Only an idiot would believe that because these facts are carefully selected to lead the listener to the (unstated) conclusion of Beck's argument.

Once you start looking for arguments by innuendo, you'll find them everywhere in politics. In the spring of 2012, a number of conservative commentators reacted to President Obama's reelection campaign theme of "Forward" by pointing out that *forward* is a word that was prominently featured in many communist publications, which is indisputably correct. Is this evidence that President Obama is a communist or has communist sympathies? Absolutely not. But it can be enough "evidence" for someone who doesn't like President Obama all that much in the first place.

Like all bad political arguments, the argument by innuendo is popular with both the right and the left. Michael Moore's *Fahrenheit 9/11*—the top-grossing documentary film of all time—is an absolute masterwork of argument by innuendo. A casual viewing of the film would understandably lead a person to believe that the Bush administration recklessly endangered American lives in the aftermath of 9/11 and pushed the country into a pointless war all for the benefit of the Saudi royal family and big corporate interests. But on closer examination, it's clear that Moore fails to actually connect the dots and instead relies on layer after layer of innuendo. His approach is made even more effective by being combined with a first-rate appeal to emotion consisting of ominous voice-overs, well-chosen music, and slick editing. Millions of people saw the film, and the critics just loved it—*Fahrenheit 9/11* earned a "certified fresh" rating on the movie metareview site Rotten Tomatoes, receiving 84 percent positive reviews. Is Michael Moore purposely misleading the American public? Well, he's an intelligent man who probably understands basic logical fallacies. And his documentaries have made him both wealthy and famous, which almost anyone would love. Can we trust Michael Moore? I don't know. I don't know.

## THE POST HOC FALLACY

When President Obama was elected in 2008, the United States imported 57 percent of its oil. Two years later, dependence on foreign oil was down to under 50 percent—the lowest it had been in 13 years. The natural conclusion to draw from this is that President Obama has done a really good job in reducing the United States' dependence on foreign oil, a conclusion the Obama campaign urged viewers to accept in its first commercial of the 2012 campaign. But according to the independent fact-checking site Politifact, the president's claim was only "half-true."[10] The Obama ad didn't lie about any of the facts, but it conveniently neglected to mention that dependence on foreign oil had been declining since 2005—four years before Obama took office. The ad also failed to mention that the recession played a big role by reducing overall demand for oil. Team Obama assumed that most of us wouldn't realize any of this and was hoping to convince us by using the post hoc fallacy.

The post hoc fallacy is more accurately the "post hoc ergo propter hoc" fallacy, which means, roughly translated from the Latin, "after this, therefore because of this."* In other words, you commit this fallacy when you assume that because A happened before B, A *caused* B. We generally won't fall for this fallacy unless the proposed cause has some plausible relationship to the effect, though there are some exceptions (such as the lucky jersey that somehow magically helps your team win).

In arguing that he's responsible for lessened dependence on foreign oil, President Obama was using the post hoc fallacy to take credit he didn't deserve. This fallacy can also be used in the opposite way, to try and convince us that we should blame someone for something that might not actually be their fault (or not entirely their fault). Here's an example, taken from an August, 2009 opinion article by Grover Norquist, president of the influential interest group Americans for Tax Reform:

President Obama demanded that Congress spend hundreds of billions of dollars to stimulate the economy. On Friday, February 13, Congress

---

*The fact that it's a Latin phrase should tell you that this bad argument has been around a long, long time.

approved a disgraceful trillion-dollar spending and debt package under the guise of economic stimulus. Since that date at least 1.5 million jobs have been lost in America. Spend more money. Have fewer jobs. Let's stop this madness.[11]

What Grover Norquist would like you to believe is that jobs have been lost because of what he called "a disgraceful trillion-dollar spending and debt package" (notice the appeal to emotion). The numbers are correct (or at least close enough) and so is the time sequence. But he doesn't offer any proof that the spending *caused* the additional job losses. It could be that other factors were responsible. It could even be that the spending prevented *even more* job losses from happening, something that many economists believe to be the case. We don't know, and Norquist doesn't even attempt to make a case, hoping instead that we won't notice he's committed the post hoc fallacy.

It's important to keep in mind that there's almost always a significant lag time between when a law is passed and when its effects are felt. This is especially true for large and complicated laws, which generally require considerable time to implement. Norquist wrote his editorial less than six months after the passage of the stimulus bill he wanted his readers to believe was counterproductive. Yet at that time, less than one-fifth of the stimulus money had been spent, meaning that the program he claims was counterproductive had barely even started.[12] For the same reason, claims made by Mitt Romney's 2012 presidential campaign about the number of jobs lost "under President Obama" were also not quite right because they counted all jobs lost starting from January 1, 2009. President Obama wasn't even inaugurated until January 20, and it was several months before job losses could be reasonably attributed to any policies the Obama administration had rushed into effect. The Romney campaign was absolutely correct in claiming that hundreds of thousands of job losses came after Obama was elected. But claiming that all of them were caused by President Obama is committing the post hoc fallacy.

Once you start looking for it, you'll find the post hoc fallacy all over the place because arguing "this happened, then that happened, so this caused that" is a lot quicker and easier than carefully considering those pesky details.

## STRAW MAN

When someone greatly oversimplifies an opposing position for the purpose of attacking it, they're committing the straw man fallacy. This happens all the time in political argument for at least two reasons. The first has to do with the nature of modern media: when you have a limited amount of time or space to grab an impatient audience, you don't want to waste it explaining your opponent's argument (especially if it's a good argument.) Second, it's a lot easier to poke holes in an abbreviated, simplified version of an argument than in the whole thing.

The straw man fallacy frequently involves using an out-of-context statement by an opponent and pretending that this represents the opponent's entire viewpoint on an issue. Take, for example, a 2012 campaign speech in which President Obama said the following about success in America:

> Look, if you've been successful, you didn't get there on your own. You didn't get there on your own. I'm always struck by people who think, well, it must be because I was just so smart. There are a lot of smart people out there. It must be because I worked harder than everybody else. Let me tell you something—there are a whole bunch of hardworking people out there.
>
> If you were successful, somebody along the line gave you some help. There was a great teacher somewhere in your life. Somebody helped to create this unbelievable American system that we have that allowed you to thrive. Somebody invested in roads and bridges. If you've got a business—you didn't build that. Somebody else made that happen. The Internet didn't get invented on its own. Government research created the Internet so that all the companies could make money off the Internet.[13]

There's not much to disagree with there. In fact, what President Obama says seems so obvious as to be hardly worth saying at all. But Obama's opponents almost immediately realized the excellent straw man they could build by focusing on a single sentence: "If you've got a business—you didn't build that." The straw man that Obama's opponents constructed from those nine words resulted in a media deluge that put Obama supporters on the defensive and dominated campaign coverage for weeks. It's also a pretty clear demonstration of how powerful this particular bad argument can be.

## FALSE ANALOGY

To make an analogy is to point out similarities or shared attributes between things (e.g., "politics is a game"). In political argument, analogies are often made between present-day politicians or programs and those of the past. This can be done in a positive way—when the person or plan is compared to some other person or plan lots of people like—or, more commonly, in a negative fashion by making the comparison with a disliked individual or program.

A false analogy is one that draws an inaccurate comparison between two things (e.g., "politics is a jelly donut"). Closely related to this is the weak analogy, in which the similarity between two things is overstated. In politics, the Hitler/Nazi comparison has become the classic false analogy and one that's used more often than you might think. The analogy between Hitler/ Nazis and some modern political figure isn't usually direct; instead, an indirect analogy is used. Glenn Beck, for instance, notes that the Obama administration's health reform law is considered progressive legislation. He then points out that some early twentieth-century progressives, President Woodrow Wilson included, were interested in eugenics—that is, methods of "improving" people through selective breeding. He then mentions that the Nazis practiced eugenics. You can fill in the last bit yourself (... therefore, Obama is kind of a Nazi). In fact, you *have to* fill it in yourself because Beck won't do it for you. The analogy is implied, making this a nice combination of two fallacies: false analogy and argument by innuendo.*

In promoting his health care legislation, President Obama frequently made an analogy to car insurance, arguing that a government requirement to carry health insurance wasn't all that unusual because people are already required to have insurance for their vehicles. But there are a few pretty important differences between health care insurance and auto insurance. Most obviously, if you don't want to be forced into buying auto insurance you can choose not to drive.† Second, the type of auto insurance that government mandates is liability insurance, which covers only damage you do to other people or their cars. You're perfectly free to not insure yourself against smashing your own car into a wall or doing whatever other dumb things you might want to do with it. President Obama's mandatory health insurance doesn't work that way because it's primarily designed to protect the insured person and not whomever the insured person might injure. The analogy between health insurance and auto insurance might sound plausible on the surface (after all, they've both got "insurance" in the name) but because of the differences between health and auto insurance, it's a weak analogy and a bad argument.

---

*If you look a little closer, you'll probably find elements of appeal to emotion, vague language, hasty generalization, and straw man as well.
†While choosing not to live is technically an option for those *truly* opposed to mandatory health care insurance, it's a pretty radical option.

## PROOF BY VERBOSITY

Proof by verbosity isn't exactly a bad argument; it's more of a great delivery mechanism for bad arguments. The idea is fairly straightforward: if you know you don't have a very good argument, you can sometimes slip it by people if you throw out enough information quickly enough to make what you're saying seem plausible on the surface. Because the information is presented so quickly, it's unlikely that most people will be able to really evaluate the argument you're making.

This, it should be obvious, is a fallacy tailor-made for television and radio. Because you can't control the pace at which the argument is being presented in these mediums, all sorts of ridiculous stuff can pass as reasoned argument. If you've ever been taken in by an infomercial for an utterly astounding product (not sold in stores!!), only to be sorely disappointed when your ShamWow or Garden Weasel didn't completely change your life, you understand how proof by verbosity works. As we've already seen, one of the great advantages of political information in print is that you get to control the pace. The writer literally can't make you go any faster than you want to. This makes it extremely difficult for this fallacy to work in print. But if your exposure to political argument is largely through television or radio, it's a good bet that you've been taken in by the proof by verbosity fallacy many times. To see this fallacy in action, all you have to do is tune in to any of the many political talk shows on MSNBC or Fox News—pay attention, and before too long, you'll have all the proof by verbosity you can handle.

## AD HOMINEM

More Latin (yay!): *ad hominem* means "to the man"; the fallacy refers to the practice of attacking a person instead of the person's argument. President George W. Bush was a frequent target of ad hominem attacks, often focusing on his alleged stupidity. Other regular targets were Vice President Cheney and presidential advisor Karl Rove, both commonly portrayed as evil geniuses (or sometimes as just plain evil). Many ad hominem attacks are disguised (or rationalized) as an analysis of character, as in "how can we trust anyone who would do that to be our congressperson/senator/president?" When the criticism involves something obviously related to politics, that's perfectly okay. For example, it's reasonable to argue that a person who embezzled from his previous employer shouldn't be trusted with public funds because that's bad behavior that pretty clearly relates to politics. But many attacks have, at best, a minor connection to politics, whether it's President Clinton being raked over the coals for having sex with an intern or Mitt Romney being called out for putting the family dog on the roof of his station wagon during a vacation trip. People certainly do all sorts of misguided and sometimes outright stupid things, but no matter how juicy they are, if they aren't related to politics they're bad political arguments.

## APPEAL TO FALSE AUTHORITY

It's unrealistic to expect people to check every single fact in every argument, and so many political arguments rely on appeals to authority. For example, in an argument concerning what should be done about unemployment, almost everyone relies on the U.S. government for unemployment data. When it comes to straightforward factual information like that, there tends to be a lot of agreement on what constitutes a good authority.

But in order to make an argument about what should or shouldn't be done in politics, you almost always have to interpret raw data. This isn't so straightforward, and while plenty of people are willing to give it a shot, not that many people have the training and experience necessary to carefully analyze information. Citing the findings of an unqualified person or organization is appealing to false authority.

You're unlikely to see very many blatant appeals to false authority; for instance, nobody is going to try to change your view on climate change by bringing up what he heard Adam Sandler say about it (at least I hope not.) The appeals to false authority that tend to get us happen when the person or organization being cited *seems* like a good authority but actually isn't. This happens a lot because oftentimes we're willing to consider someone an authority based on extremely limited information. For instance, many people assume that if a person has a Ph.D. after their name or is affiliated with a prestigious university or institute, this person must be an expert. But that's not necessarily so. People with advanced degrees in political science almost always specialize in one very small part of their field and won't necessarily know anything more than an educated layperson when it comes to the vast spectrum of politics that lies outside their area of expertise. For example, I've got a Ph.D. in political science, but my training was in U.S. politics—all I know about international politics is what I read online. Assuming that a Ph.D. in political science means that someone knows all about every kind of politics is like assuming that a podiatrist is qualified to remove your gall bladder.

It's important to keep in mind why "experts" get chosen to be in the media in the first place. While having an impressive-sounding degree or résumé is often a basic requirement, what's really important to reporters and interviewers is the expert's willingness and ability to say interesting things. The better you are at being interesting, the more attractive you are to the media. But there's no reason to think that the most interesting people are the most expert experts. In fact, there's some evidence to suggest just the opposite. Psychologist Philip Tetlock has made a careful study of expert authority, reporting on his results in the book *Expert Political Judgment: How Good Is It? How Can We Know?* Tetlock found that there is, in fact, a relationship between how well known an expert is and the quality of that expert's opinions. The problem is that it's an *inverse* relationship, which means that the better known experts are, the *worse* they tend to be at predicting what will happen in politics.[14] From the so-called expert's point of view, there's a big plus for making bold claims—getting media exposure—but no penalty for being wrong because in a few days, almost nobody will even remember what some guy on TV said about the deficit or who was going to win the election.

Because reporters are nearly always on tight deadlines, they can't afford to exhaustively search out top authorities and hope that these actual experts will return their calls or answer their e-mail before a story is due. What often happens is that a reporter will contact a local university looking for someone with a Ph.D. who is willing to talk. A lot of Ph.Ds. enjoy seeing their names in print and their faces on TV (just like normal people), and so even if they're not actual experts, they might end up giving a reporter a quote or agreeing to come down to the studio to film a segment for the local news.

There are times when expert opinion can shed valuable light on a political issue, but there are plenty of nonexpert experts out there, and even the true experts in the media often don't do such a great job. This doesn't mean you should ignore expert opinion, but it's a good idea to keep in mind all of the reasons these experts end up being chosen by the media in the first place.

## FALSE DICHOTOMY

"You're either with us or against us." "America: love it or leave it." "A vote for Bush is a vote for war." What all these simple arguments have in common is that they present us with a choice between two options. But if you think about it, you'll probably realize that they aren't the only two options available and that the real choice is more complex. That's the false dichotomy fallacy (sometimes called false choice or false dilemma)—getting people to falsely believe that there are only two possible choices. Because black-or-white thinking is simpler and less mentally taxing than consideration of all viable options, the false dichotomy is a regular feature of political argument. But in real life, things are almost never as clear as they appear in the bumper-sticker and sound-bite friendly world of the false dichotomy.

A more savvy way to employ this bad argument for political ends is to claim that *everyone else* is talking about one of two dramatically opposed choices, but you, in your enormous wisdom, are calling for a sensible middle path between these extremes. President Obama is a master practitioner of this, having called for rejecting false choices between "our safety and our ideals,"[15] between "paying down our deficits ... and investing in job creation and economic growth,"[16] and between "clean air, clean water, and growing the economy."[17] He's right in pointing out these false choices, but in pretending that they are choices that his opponents are seriously advocating, President Obama is making some bad arguments in order to score political points.

## SLIPPERY SLOPE

This is the "the next thing you know" argument, as in, "Let gays get married and the next thing you know, people will be marrying their pets." In the last few years, the most prominent political slippery slope argument has been about a perilous path that could lead to mandatory broccoli (*shudder*). The argument—if the government can make us buy health insurance, the next thing you know, they'll force us to buy broccoli—even made it to the U.S. Supreme Court, where it was raised by Justice Scalia.[18] Sometimes, one thing really does lead to another in a clear and logical sequence. It only becomes a bad argument when the person making it doesn't explain why doing something makes something else more likely. Because it's quicker and easier to not focus on those tedious but important middle steps, many people simply leave them out. Maybe requiring mandatory health insurance really *is* the first inevitable step on a road that ends with government agents force-feeding us broccoli, but if you simply assert this without explaining how we're likely to get from here to there, you're making a bad argument.

## ARGUMENT FROM IGNORANCE

Despite how it might sound, this bad argument isn't about appealing to the ignorance of the public or making an argument when you don't know what you're talking about. The argument from ignorance is when someone says that "if you can't prove me wrong, I must be right." This is a favorite tactic of the political interview. Fox's Bill O'Reilly, for example, regularly uses it on his guests by stating his position and then challenging his guests to "tell me where I'm wrong." By doing this, he makes his view the standard that must be disproven; otherwise, the implication is that he must be right. This can be very useful because on the surface it suggests that the person making the argument is actually interested in understanding opposing views rather than in just having his position affirmed; however, what he's really doing is cleverly positioning his view as the truth that should be accepted until decisively disproven. That puts his opponents on the defensive, and because it's really difficult to construct an argument in a live interview, he comes out on top nearly every time, not because he has the better argument but because he's skillfully using a bad argument.

## BADNESS ABOUNDS

As we've seen, there are plenty of ways that political arguments go bad. Sometimes this is due to the limitations of political media itself—putting together a good political argument often takes time and expertise that overburdened media analysts simply don't have. Not only is it much easier to not bother with constructing a logically sound argument, it's often not good for business. As we've seen, many Americans aren't nearly as interested in good arguments as they are in arguments that confirm their beliefs. As a general rule, it's good to be a little suspicious of any political argument. After all, most people who make political arguments have some sort of agenda, as opposed to being disinterested seekers of the truth.* Before you accept their arguments—particularly if those arguments are short and simple—take a minute to ask yourself if they're making a generally solid case or if you're being asked to buy into yet another bad argument.

## NOTES

1. Rush Limbaugh, "Barack Obama Hates This Country," *The Rush Limbaugh Show*, July 16, 2012, http://www.rushlimbaugh.com/daily/2012/07/16/barack_obama_hates_this_country.

2. Markos Moulitsas, "Can Romney Interact with Anyone without Insulting Them?" Daily Kos, July 26, 2012, http://www.dailykos.com/story/2012/07/26/1113912/-Can-Romney-interact-with-ANYONE-without-insulting-them.

3. Jeff Zeleny, "Obama Campaign Takes Gamble in Going Negative," *The New York Times*, July 28, 2012, http://www.nytimes.com/2012/07/29/us/politics/obama-campaign-takes-gamble-in-going-negative.html.

*Except for me, of course. I am an utterly disinterested seeker of the truth.

4. "Obama for America TV Ad: 'Firms,' " accessed December 21, 2012, http://www.youtube.com/watch?v=Ud3mMj0AZZk&feature=youtube_gdata_player.

5. "Where Did All The Money Go?" accessed September 10, 2012, http://www.youtube.com/watch?v=N77kBx5KZqo.

6. Richard R. Lau, Lee Sigelman, and Ivy Brown Rovner, "The Effects of Negative Political Campaigns: A Meta-Analytic Reassessment," *Journal of Politics* 69, no. 4 (2007): 1176–1209.

7. "Top Bush Officials Push Case against Saddam," CNN, September 8, 2002, http://articles.cnn.com/2002-09-08/politics/iraq.debate_1_nuclear-weapons-top-nuclear-scientists-aluminum-tubes?_s=PM:ALLPOLITICS.

8. Jeffery M. Jones, "Public Support for Iraq Invasion Inches Upward," Gallup, March 17, 2003, http://www.gallup.com/poll/7990/public-support-iraq-invasion-inches-upward.aspx.

9. Mark Leibovich, "Being Glenn Beck," *New York Times*, September 29, 2010, http://www.nytimes.com/2010/10/03/magazine/03beck-t.html?_r=3&pagewanted=all.

10. "Barack Obama Campaign Says U.S. Dependence on Foreign Oil Now Below 50 Percent," *PolitiFact Ohio*, January 26, 2012, http://www.politifact.com/ohio/statements/2012/jan/26/barack-obama/barack-obama-campaign-says-us-dependence-foreign-o/.

11. Grover Norquist, "Happy Cost of Government Day," Fox News, August 11, 2009, http://www.foxnews.com/opinion/2009/08/11/happy-cost-government-day/.

12. "The Economic Impact of the American Recovery and Reinvestment Act of 2009 First Quarterly Report," The White House, September 10, 2009, http://www.whitehouse.gov/administration/eop/cea/Economic-Impact/.

13. Brian Montopoli, "Unpacking the 'You Didn't Build That' Debate," *CBS News*, July 24, 2012, http://www.cbsnews.com/8301-503544_162-57478808-503544/unpacking-the-you-didnt-build-that-debate/.

14. Philip E. Tetlock, *Expert Political Judgment: How Good Is It? How Can We Know?* (Princeton, NJ: Princeton University Press, 2006).

15. "Barack Obama's Inaugural Address," *New York Times*, January 20, 2009, http://www.nytimes.com/2009/01/20/us/politics/20text-obama.html.

16. Ari Shapiro, "Obama's Libya Doctrine Vague amid False Choices," NPR, April 2, 2011, http://www.npr.org/2011/04/02/135064837/obamas-libya-doctrine-vague-amid-false-choices.

17. Rebecca Leber, "Obama: We Don't Have to 'Make a Choice between Having Clean Air and Clean Water and Growing This Economy,' " Thinkprogress, January 10, 2012, http://thinkprogress.org/climate/2012/01/10/401947/obama-we-dont-have-to-make-a-choice-between-having-clean-air-and-clean-water-and-growing-this-economy/.

18. Byron Tau, "Scalia Wonders about a Broccoli Mandate," Politico, March 27, 2012, http://www.politico.com/politico44/2012/03/scalia-wonders-about-a-broccoli-mandate-118823.html.

# SEVEN

## Misleading Numbers

Most of us are comfortable dealing with simple, everyday math—addition, subtraction, multiplication, and even some basic division—but that's just about as far as our mathematical comfort zone extends. As we've already seen, millions of people don't possess the level of literacy necessary to read the news. Mathematical literacy may be an even bigger problem: Only 13 percent of Americans are proficient in quantitative literacy (the ability to understand and use numbers) according to a report by the National Center for Education Statistics.[1] This means that the vast majority of us are ill prepared to deal with the profusion of numbers that accompany political news and opinion.

Because of this, we are vulnerable to numerical manipulation, something that can happen not only to media consumers but even to the journalists covering the news. While we may like to think that the numbers speak for themselves, that's simply not the case much of the time. It often takes a little bit of digging to really understand what numbers are (or aren't) telling us—digging that the media generally doesn't bother doing. As Scott Adams, the creator of *Dilbert*, puts it, "Reporters are faced with the daily choice of painstakingly researching stories or writing whatever people tell them. Both approaches pay the same."[2]

### CHECKING SOURCES

The numbers that are used in political arguments are almost never simply made up out of thin air, which means that at some point some person or, more likely, some group of people collected, organized, and published a big bunch of raw data. As with any human activity, data collection is subject to error, both intentional and unintentional. And so the first question you should ask when you see *any* political data is, "Where did it come from?" If the people responsible for the data have a clear agenda, and their analysis just happens to support that agenda, you should definitely give their numbers a closer look. If, for example, you're interested in the facts about gun control laws and gun violence, the National Rifle Association will be happy to give you all sorts of data that proves guns can make us safer. Or you could check with the Brady Campaign to Prevent Gun Violence, which has its own data that will prove just the opposite.

The next question you should ask yourself is, "*How* was the data collected?" Finding this out can be as simple as checking for a link to additional information on the data source, something that many political news sites include. At a minimum, reputable political news sources will give you enough information about their source material so that you can find out more on your own, often with just a quick Google search. Be very suspicious of any news source that uses political data without clearly telling you where it came from.

Because you won't generally have the time (or interest) to check into sources for yourself, here's a general rule of thumb about political numbers: Data from federal and state government sources is almost always reliable, which is why it's so commonly cited by politicians, interest groups, and media organizations all across the political spectrum. Data collected by researchers from academic institutions is also pretty solid because much of their work is subject to peer review, a process by which experts in a field check on each other's work. When it comes to public opinion data, major media outlets, as well as a top-tier polling organizations like Gallup, Roper, and the Pew Research Center, do a very respectable job of data gathering. View any other sources—including political parties, think tanks (which usually have an ideological agenda), and candidates—with caution.

Even if you're dealing with a perfectly credible source (or a source you've decided is good enough) you still need to consider how fresh the data is. Unfortunately, there's no clear standard for determining when numbers go bad because it depends on the particular circumstances. In order to determine whether data is still reasonably fresh, ask yourself how soon it's likely to change. In some instances things can move very quickly, such as in election polls, where a candidate can have a big lead at one point only to be trailing a month or two later. On the other hand, there are things like population data, where information that's several years old might be just fine. There are also plenty of instances in which the most recent source of data is older than you'd like—sometimes a *lot* older—but there's nothing newer that you can trust.* In that case, you work with what you have, keeping in mind that any conclusions drawn from old data will probably be less solid than if you had more recent information.

## THE SQUISHY DEFINITIONS BEHIND HARD DATA

What does it mean to be unemployed? Being without a job, obviously. But if you take a few minutes to think about unemployment, you'll see it's not as clear cut as you might have initially imagined. What about teenagers, for instance—a lot of them work, but plenty don't, so should they count toward unemployment totals? How about people who aren't looking for work, or those who've given up looking? And what do we do with people who are only working part-time—is it fair to count them the same as those who are working full-time? Should we count part-time workers who have failed to find full-time employment the same as part-timers who don't want full-time jobs? How about older people? Many retire voluntarily, but plenty are essentially forced into retirement.

The unemployment numbers that virtually everyone in politics use comes from the U.S. Department of Labor's Bureau of Labor Statistics (BLS), the official government source for unemployment data. Here's their definition of unemployed: "Persons are classified as unemployed if they do not have a job, have actively looked for work in the prior 4 weeks, and are currently available for work."[3] Why four weeks? Because the people at BLS responsible for making the definition decided that if you haven't looked for a job in a month, you're not *really* trying to look for a job. There's no particular reason that it couldn't be three or five weeks—four weeks happens to be a month, which probably seemed like a nice cutoff point. That's pretty subjective. Another problem with this definition is that it doesn't count all the people who want to work but give up in frustration after a month of no success, or who settle for part-time employment, especially in a bad economy. It turns out that there are quite a few of these people, and an unemployment rate that includes them is a lot higher than the standard measure: 13.9 percent, versus 7.7 percent for the official unemployment rate (as of November 2012).[4] Of course, the government wants unemployment to appear as low as possible, and so it's understandable that the official figure would be the one that makes unemployment look like less of a problem. This

---

*For instance, my data source for the "only 13 percent of Americans are proficient in quantitative literacy" factoid comes from a survey conducted back in 2003. That's pretty old, but it's the most recent credible, nationwide study of adult mathematical literacy out there.

doesn't mean that this official unemployment rate is wrong, just that it's an artificial and subjective measure, as any measure of unemployment has to be to a certain extent.

That's only the tip of the definitional iceberg. To get a full understanding of how unemployment is defined and measured, you would need to review BLS's full explanation, which runs to more than 5,500 words—about eight pages if you printed it out.[5] The point is that there are an awful lot of judgment calls that go into the construction of political statistics. Ideally, we would look into what goes into all of these numbers, but the reality is that we're not going to do that most of the time. But one thing we can do is keep in mind that seemingly objective numbers are based on a lot of subjective decisions.

## ABOUT AVERAGE(S)

"The average" might be the most commonly used term in data analysis, but what many people don't realize is that there are actually two basic averages, each of which provides somewhat different information about the middle in a group of numbers. The first is what statisticians call the mean. This is the number you get when you add up all the individual values of something and then divide by the number of things you have. For instance, if you wanted the mean age of U.S. senators, you'd add up all of the individual senators' ages and then divide that total by 100, which is the number of U.S. senators. The number you'd end up with—63.17 (as of 2012)—would be the mean. When you think of "the average" it's probably the mean that you're thinking about.

The mean is one sort of middle—the arithmetic center. Another type of middle is the point at which half the values are larger and half are smaller. That's what's known of as the median. A lot of the time, the mean and the median are fairly similar—for example, the median age of U.S. senators is 62.5, compared to the mean of 63.17. The only time you're likely to see a sizable difference between mean and median values is when there are some particularly large or small numbers in a group. For instance, let's say that a 90-year-old billionaire—we'll call him Rupert Mandrake—marries a 21-year-old exotic dancer named Fantasia. Fantasia has three children—twins Tiffany and Tyler, who are both 3 years old, and baby Tonya, who just turned 1. That makes the mean age of the Mandrakes 23.6, but the *median* age is only 12 because Rupert's oldness pulls up the mean value. (Why is 12 the median, when nobody in the family is actually 12 years old? Because 12 is the number exactly halfway between 3 and 21, the two middle ages in the family.) Neither of these measures of the middle is inherently better or worse than the other—they just tell us different things.

The Mandrake example brings out another important point about averages—they can conceal as much as they reveal. If the only information you have about the Mandrakes is that their mean age is 23.6, you probably aren't picturing a really old guy, a young woman, two toddlers, and a baby. But if you also know the median age of the family, you can reasonably conclude that there's probably an old Mandrake in the bunch responsible for yanking up that mean value.

In politics, this can sometimes make a big difference. "Average" household income is a good example. In 2010, the mean household income in the United States was $67,530, which doesn't sound all that shabby. But half of all American households had an income that doesn't come close to that figure, something you'd only realize if you knew that the median household income was just $49,445.[6] The reason that the mean is so much higher than the median in this case is because a small number of high-income households are pulling it way up—the mean income level for the top 20 percent of American households was almost $170,000 in 2010, which is a long way from that overall mean of under $50,000. It's the same story for unemployment: The average length of unemployment is 19 weeks if you're looking at the median, but it shoots all the way up to 40 weeks—more than double—when you look at the mean.[7]

## SPREADING OUT THE NUMBERS

If you don't want to be misled by averages, it's good to know a little bit about the spread of a group of numbers, something statisticians call data distribution. There are a number of advanced statistical methods for quantifying distributions of data, but thankfully we don't need to go into things like "standard deviation" or "quartile coefficient of dispersion" for an understanding of how a bunch of numbers spread out. In many cases, it's not all that difficult to find basic data distributions already precompiled, most commonly in the form of quartiles (four equal slices, with each being 25 percent of the total) or quintiles (five equal slices, each 20 percent of the total).

The household income data I used to illustrate the difference between mean and median is a good example. From it, we already know two important things about household income—the mean ($67,530) and the median ($49,445). Without knowing anything else, it would be understandable if we concluded that most households in the United States earn somewhere between $50,000 and $70,000 per year. But if we dig a little deeper and look at the distribution of household income (which the Census Bureau thought-fully breaks down into quintiles) we'd get a very different picture of things. The quintile distribution tells us that the bottom 20 percent of Americans averaged just over $11,000 per year. While the next 20 percent did consider-ably better, their average of $28,600 is still pretty low. That's a full 40 per-cent of the population well outside of our averages. The same is true of the top 40 percent of Americans, who had an average household income of slightly over $124,000.* Only 2 out of 10 Americans—the middle fifth of the distribution—actually fell within the household income averages. If we only look at the averages, it's entirely reasonable for us to think that most Americans are doing pretty well. But when we break it down and take a look at how the numbers spread out, we see that there are an awful lot of families doing much better, and much worse, than the averages alone suggest. If you think most Americans are doing okay economically, you're going to have very different ideas about politics than you would if you find major dispar-ities in income equality. That's one really good reason for knowing some-thing about data distribution.

## CONTEXT IS IMPORTANT

Most political numbers we see in the media are snapshots of a particular point in time. They can be really useful, but only when placed in the proper context. If we know that the unemployment rate in the United States is 7.7 percent, there's no way to decide whether that's good or bad without considering what the rate has been in the past. Put another way, looking at trends in numbers over time tells us a lot more than any particular number because it provides us with that much-needed context.

For instance, maybe you think that 7.7 percent unemployment seems really high. However, the only way to know how high 7.7 percent really is is to con-sider this number in historical context, which we get in Figure 7.1.[8]

From this, it's reasonable to conclude that, yes, 7.7 percent *is* kind of high, at least based on the standard of the last 10 years. Considering the cur-rent unemployment rate in this context might even make that 7.7 percent fig-ure seem worse than you initially thought it was. But is 10 years enough context? If we go back even further, we get a better historical feel for what 7.7 percent unemployment means, as you can see in Figure 7.2.

---

*In case you were wondering, the fourth-fifth averaged $79,040, while the highest fifth was all the way up at $169,633. The Census Bureau also reports the average for the top 5 percent, which as you might expect, is considerably higher: $287,686.

**Figure 7.1.   U.S. Unemployment from 2002 to 2012**

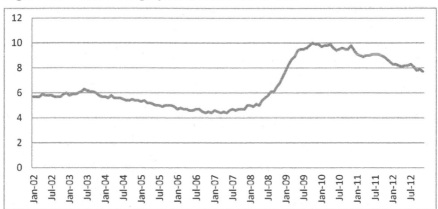

This extended historical look puts things in greater perspective: while the current unemployment rate is pretty high, it's clearly not unprecedented. The last comparable rate, in the early 1980s, was followed by relatively long periods of comparatively low unemployment. This doesn't mean that we should conclude that everything will be just fine (that, as you know, would be a hasty generalization), but it certainly gives us a more complete picture of the situation than just knowing what the current unemployment number is. The media often fail to give us this context, which can make a big difference in how we understand and interpret what's going on in the world today.

**Figure 7.2.   U.S. Unemployment from 1950 to 2012**

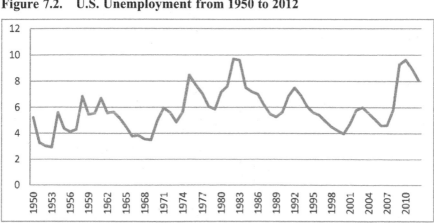

## COLLAPSING CATEGORIES

Another common problem with the political statistics seen in the media is that they're usually overall values, which may not reflect important subcategories that can provide us with a better sense of a situation. For example, the unemployment number most frequently mentioned in the media is the *national* mean (average) of 7.7 percent (as of November 2012). While this number isn't as deceptive as the 23.6 average age was for the Mandrake family, it still hides a lot of variation. For example, while unemployment may be at 7.7 percent nationally, things are a lot better in North Dakota, where the unemployment rate is 3.1 percent. And things are a lot worse in Nevada, which has an unemployment rate of 11.5 percent.[9] But there's a lot of variation even within Nevada—people in Esmeralda County, Nevada (4.7 percent unemployment), are facing a far different situation than those in Lyon County, with its 14 percent unemployment rate. You'll rarely see useful breakdowns like this in the media because the national averages the media rely on are the easiest thing to report.

## APPLES TO ORANGES: INAPPROPRIATE COMPARISONS

In making comparisons with numbers, it's important to be sure that we're comparing equivalent things. There are plenty of inappropriate "apples-to-oranges" comparisons in politics, though they're generally subtle enough that most people don't catch them.

One common inappropriate comparison involves not adjusting dollar values for inflation. This is important because over time wages and prices rise, meaning that a dollar today is worth less than it was in the past. The federal government keeps track of inflation in a number of ways, with the Consumer Price Index (CPI) being the most well-known measure. Using calculations based on the CPI, it's fairly simple to make basic adjustments for inflation.* Comparisons that adjust for inflation will make note of this, usually by indicating that values are in "real dollars" or by telling you the year to which the dollar values have been inflation- adjusted (for example, a chart might say "in 2012 dollars"). If there hasn't been an adjustment for inflation, you might see the label "constant dollars," "nominal dollars," or, more commonly, no label at all.

Adjusting for inflation can make a big difference, and the further back we go in time the bigger the difference is going to be. Let's say we want to find out if American families are doing better economically now than

---

*There are a bunch of CPI calculators available online. The official model is at the U.S. Bureau of Labor Statistics: http://data.bls.gov/cgi-bin/cpicalc.pl.

in the past. A quick look at household income over time might lead us to believe that the answer is an unqualified yes. According to BLS data, median household income in 1990 was $29,000. Two decades later it had risen to almost $50,445—an increase of over 65 percent. But because of inflation, that $29,000 from 1990 was worth $48,423 in 2010 dollars. For a real comparison over time, $48,423 is the number we need to use. When we take that instead of the non-inflation-adjusted value, we find something very different: inflation-adjusted median family income has only increased by $1,022 over two decades—barely over 2 percent. Based on this, it seems like instead of clearly improving over time, average household income has nearly stood still.

Another common apples-to-oranges comparison is between populations of different sizes. For example, plenty of people believe that big cities are particularly dangerous. If you looked at recent homicide statistics comparing New York City and Buffalo, you might conclude they have a point: in 2011, there were 515 homicides in New York City, and only 36 in Buffalo.[10] We can see this difference in graphic form in Figure 7.3.

On the face of it, we might be tempted to conclude that Buffalo is a lot safer. But when we take into consideration that New York City has a population of about 8.2 million compared to Buffalo's 262,484, the picture looks considerably different. The way to make a fair apples-to-apples comparison is to look at the per capita homicide rate (number of homicides divided by city population). Do that and you get the result seen in Figure 7.4.

The lesson here should be clear: when making comparisons, size *does* matter.

It's also important to make sure that any numbers being compared are from equivalent time periods. For instance, in a speech in the summer of

**Figure 7.3.    Homicides in Buffalo and New York City (2011)**

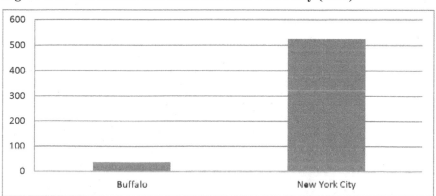

**Figure 7.4.    Homicides per Capita in Buffalo and New York City (2011)**

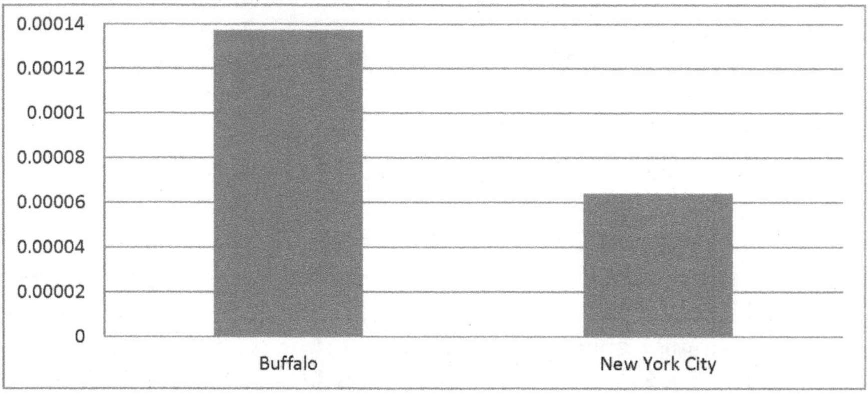

2012, President Obama told an audience in Cleveland, "Our businesses have gone back to basics and created over 4 million jobs in the last 27 months—more private sector jobs than were created during the entire seven years before the crisis."[11] That seems pretty impressive: more jobs created in a little over two years under Obama than over the entire eight years of the Bush administration.* But why "the last 27 months"? Well, it just so happens that the last 27 months coincides with the best sustained period of job creation during President Obama's time in office. A fairer comparison would pit President Obama's best 27 months against President Bush's best 27 months. Do that, and you discover that their job creation numbers are almost identical.[12] But although "my best 27 months is just about the same as President Bush's best 27 months" may be a more appropriate comparison, it's not exactly going to bring an Obama crowd to its feet.

## DECEPTIVE DISPLAYS

Charts and graphs are extremely useful because they can present a lot of information in a way that seems easy to understand.† Plus, they're almost always more eye-catching than a plain list of numbers. Because of this, a lot of political data is presented in graphical format. But visual displays can often be rigged to either exaggerate or minimize differences between

---

*If at this point you're screaming "post hoc fallacy!" congratulations. If, on the other hand, you have no idea what I mean, take another look at Chapter 6.
†If you've ever wondered what the difference is between a chart and a graph, you're not alone. There are plenty of different views on this. Here's a simple way to remember the difference: picture = chart, line = graph.

**Figure 7.5.    Top Tax Rate If Bush Tax Cuts Expire (Fox Business Y Axis)**

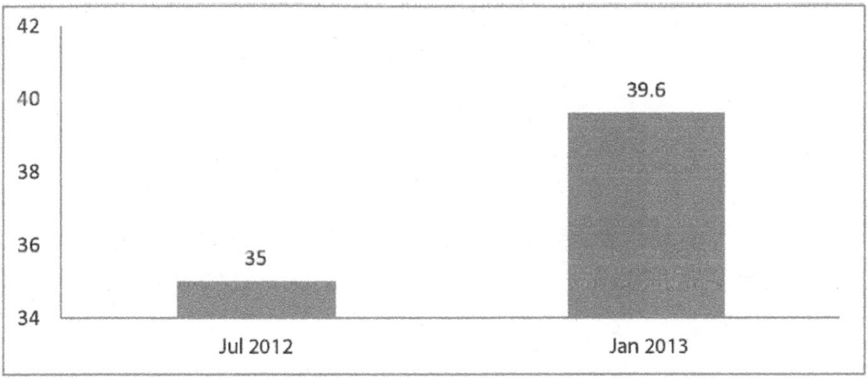

things through what's technically known as manipulating the Y axis (that's the up-and-down one[*]). For example, when the Fox Business channel wanted to show viewers what would happen to the top tax rate if the Bush tax cuts were allows to expire, they showed a chart that looked like the one you see in Figure 7.5.

Looking at that chart, you'd understandably come to the conclusion that expiration of the Bush tax cuts will lead to a massive increase in the top tax rate. While the numbers over each bar tell you that the actual change will be 4.6 percent, what you *see* (which is what the Fox Business audience also saw, though their graph was much spiffier) is the over 500 percent difference in the height of the bars—a whole lot more than the 4.6 percent *actual* difference. The Fox Business numbers are absolutely correct, but by starting the Y axis at 34 and ending it at 42 they greatly increase our perception of the change. If we use the exact same numbers but alter the Y axis so that it runs from 0 to 100 percent, things look a whole lot different, as we can see in Figure 7.6.

Another common way of distorting visual displays of data is to show only the part of a trend that supports your position, as we saw with the unemployment data graphs earlier in this chapter. Political campaigns and partisan news sources do this all the time. One recent example is a graph the Obama campaign posted in August 2012 that displayed the president's record on job creation. The graph relies on the same BLS data that Fox News, the Romney campaign, and everyone else does, but only a carefully selected portion of it.

---

*If you can't remember which one is the Y axis and which one is the X axis, try this (it worked for me): Y is for yawn, and when you yawn your mouth moves up and down, just like the Y axis.

**Figure 7.6.   Top Tax Rate If Bush Tax Cuts Expire (0-100 Y Axis)**

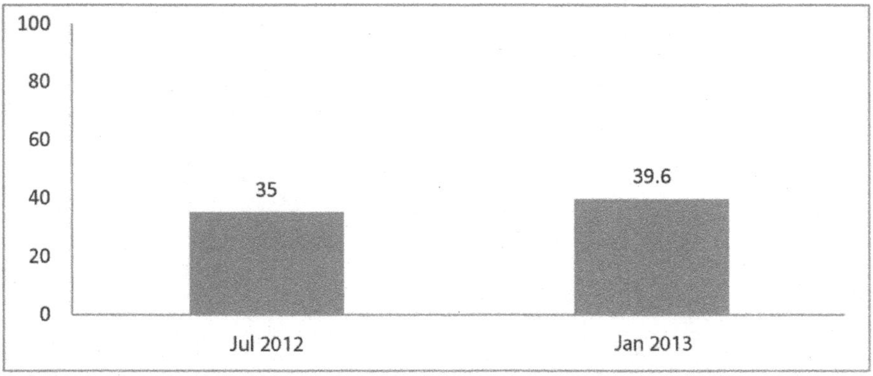

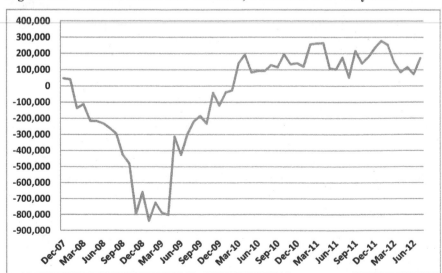

The message you're expected to take away from the graph, which Figure 7.7 recreates using the same BLS data, is clear: President Bush ran the economy into a deep ditch, a ditch President Obama has successfully pulled us out of.

You might have noticed that the graph starts in December 2007, which may seem like a pretty random place to begin. After all, that only covers the final 13 months of the eight-year Bush presidency, as compared to all 42 months Obama has been president. You might also have noticed that during the Bush administration part of the graph, the line sinks like a stone. But if we look at the months of the Bush presidency the Obama graph

**Figure 7.7.   Private-Sector Job Creation, December 2007-July 2012**

**Figure 7.8.   Private Sector Job Creation, January 2001-July 2012**

*doesn't* show, the simple story the Obama campaign is trying to sell us becomes considerably more complex, as you can see in Figure 7.8.

All of a sudden, the reason why the Obama campaign started its graph where it did becomes fairly obvious—it showed job creation under President Bush in the most negative light possible. But based on the overall data from the BLS, you could make an argument that the numbers under President Bush are considerably better than under Obama: 147,000 jobs created under Bush, and 507,000 jobs *lost* under Obama. That's a graph you'll never see on any pro-Obama site.

## NUMBERS: USEFUL BUT TRICKY

Whenever you see any sort of number associated with politics, keep in mind that while it may give you some useful information, it's only one part of a bigger picture. Also remember that those numbers didn't just fall out of the sky but are the result of a bunch of decisions made by imperfect human beings using subjective methods. Charts and graphs based on these numbers can be extremely useful tools for showing you what's going on in the world of politics, but they can also be extremely useful tools for misleading you, and so you shouldn't always trust your eyes. Because numbers seem so solid to many of us, they carry with them a certain authority. But as we've seen, political numbers can be misleading, and accepting them at face value can give you a very skewed view of reality.

## NOTES

1. "National Assessment of Adult Literacy (NAAL)," National Center for Education Statistics, accessed December 21, 2012, http://nces.ed.gov/naal/kf _demographics.asp.

2. Scott Adams, *The Dilbert Principle: A Cubicle's-Eye View of Bosses, Meetings, Management Fads & Other Workplace Afflictions* (New York: Harper Paperbacks, 1997), 83.

3. "How the Government Measures Unemployment," Bureau of Labor Statistics, accessed December 21, 2012, http://www.bls.gov/cps/cps_htgm.htm.

4. Employment data from Bureau of Labor Statistics, accessed December 21, 2012, "Employment Situation Summary Table A," http://www.bls.gov/news .release/empsit.a.htm, and "Table A-15. Alternative Measures of Labor Under-utilization," http://www.bls.gov/news.release/empsit.t15.htm.

5. "How the Government Measures Unemployment."

6. All household income data in this chapter from U.S. Bureau of Census, accessed June 6, 2012, http://www.census.gov/hhes/www/income/data/historical/ household/.

7. Unemployment data from November 2012, as reported by the Federal Reserve Economic Data service of the Federal Reserve Bank of St. Louis, accessed December 10, 2012, http://research.stlouisfed.org/fred2/series/UEMPMED (median) and http://research.stlouisfed.org/fred2/series/UEMPMEAN (mean).

8. "Google Public Data," accessed December 18, 2012, http://www.google .com/publicdata?ds=usunemployment&met=unemployment_rate&tdim=true &dl=en&hl=en&q=united+states+unemployment+rate.

9. All unemployment data from "Local Area Unemployment Statistics," Bureau of Labor Statistics, accessed December 10, 2012, http://www.bls.gov/ lau/home.htm/.

10. Buffalo and New York City crime data from "Crime in the United States by Metropolitan Statistical Area, 2011," Federal Bureau of Investigation, accessed December 10, 2012, http://www.fbi.gov/about-us/cjis/ucr/crime-in -the-u.s/2011/crime-in-the-u.s.-2011/tables/table-6.

11. "Remarks by the President on the Economy—Cleveland, OH," The White House, June 14, 2012, http://www.whitehouse.gov/the-press-office/2012/ 06/14/remarks-president-economy-cleveland-oh.

12. "Obama's Economic Sleight of Hand," FactCheck.org, June 15, 2012, http://factcheck.org/2012/06/obamas-economic-sleight-of-hand/.

# EIGHT

## "Survey Says . . .": Problems with Polls

*Public opinion in this country is everything.*

—Abraham Lincoln

*There is no such thing as public opinion. There is only published opinion.*

—Winston Churchill

Politicians have always cared about what the public thinks, which is why public opinion polling of some sort has been going on for as long as there's been politics. As far back as ancient Babylonia, leaders engaged in a sort of opinion polling—putting on disguises and walking the streets to hear what the people were talking about. While these haphazard opinion polls may not have been very accurate, they demonstrate that getting a feel for the public mood has always been important, even in societies that were anything but democratic. Although most rulers throughout history didn't have to worry about getting voted out of office (being a king has its advantages), the threat of a disgruntled populace rising up and doing far worse than electing someone else was always present. And so for most of recorded history having a sense of public opinion wasn't just smart politics—it was a survival skill (often literally).

Over time democratic government expanded, a development that gave the people a greater voice in choosing their leaders and policies. The spread of democracy also made those leaders—as well as their political opponents—even more concerned with figuring out what the people wanted. But until the 1930s, a lot of public opinion polling wasn't all that far removed from what those Babylonian leaders did. Polling typically involved going somewhere a bunch of people would gather, asking questions to whomever would talk, and then compiling all the replies. These early opinion surveys, often called "straw polls,"* were often way off even when lots of people were polled because certain parts of the population would be under- or overrepresented. If, for example, a polling organization got most of its information from people in public places, they might miss a lot of older citizens who weren't able to get out as easily. Or a poll taken mainly from people who were out during working hours would yield different results than one gathered from a crowd enjoying a weekend at the beach. And as populations got larger and more diverse, the problems of over- and underrepresentation only increased.

The biggest polling failure in U.S. history resulted from an attempt to poll an extremely large and diverse group – the population of the United States. A popular national weekly magazine called the *Literary Digest* (a sort of forerunner to *Time* magazine) had been conducting presidential election polls since 1920. The people running the *Literary Digest* poll realized the inherent difficulty in accurately representing such a large group, and so they decided to go big (and expensive) by mailing out millions of surveys to potential voters. Understanding that under- or overrepresentation might be a problem even with so many surveys, they used telephone listings and motor vehicle registration records from across the country to randomly select the people to whom the questions would be mailed. This was a massive undertaking, especially in precomputer days, but it had produced good results in the past: the *Literary Digest* poll correctly picked the winner in all four presidential elections from 1920 to 1932.† The 1936 poll was the magazine's biggest ever, with over 10 million ballots mailed out and 2 million returned. The *Literary Digest*'s team of number crunchers carefully compiled this mass of data and announced their findings shortly before the election: Republican Alf Landon would win 55 percent of the vote, soundly defeating the incumbent, Franklin Roosevelt, who was expected to be the choice of only 41 percent of voters (a decrease of over 16 percent from his total of four

---

*The term comes from the old practice of throwing a handful of straw in the air to see which way the wind was blowing. Today, the term *straw poll* is mainly used in reference to nonbinding presidential preference votes held at state-level political party conventions.
†Though that may seem more impressive than it actually is—the closest presidential election over that period was still a wipeout: Herbert Hoover's 1928 victory, in which he won 17.4 percent more of the popular vote than challenger Al Smith.

years earlier). As you probably know, this was a very bad prediction. FDR didn't just win reelection in 1936; he cruised past Landon, getting over 60 percent of the popular vote—nearly 20 percent more than the *Literary Digest* had predicted. The magazine was hugely embarrassed by its major miscall, which was thought to be at least partially responsible for its ceasing publication in 1938 (though the Great Depression might have played a role too).

How could the *Literary Digest* have screwed up so badly? A number of analyses concluded that the problem was in the telephone directories and auto registration lists the *Literary Digest* used for its survey mailings. People who could afford phones and cars turned out not to be representative of the country as a whole, especially during a time of substantial economic hardship. In 1936, only 33 percent of the population had telephones, and even fewer—just 22 percent—owned cars. People with phones and cars were much more likely to vote Republican, leaving phoneless, carless, FDR-supporting voters underrepresented in the *Literary Digest*'s poll.

The main lesson of the *Literary Digest* fiasco is that no matter how large a group of people you survey, there's always the possibility that it won't accurately represent the entire population. In 1935, a statistician named George Gallup realized that by using his knowledge of statistical probability, he could not only predict election results more accurately than the *Literary Digest* but he could do it with a much smaller sample group and at a fraction of the cost. Gallup's first test came in the 1936 presidential election, where he picked FDR to win reelection with 55.7 percent of the popular vote. While Gallup was a bit off on the final margin—Roosevelt ended up getting 62.5 percent of the vote—he did a lot better than the massive *Literary Digest* poll. And Gallup got his results not by surveying millions of people but by conducting only a few thousand interviews.

Gallup's scientific approach to polling clearly worked, and time showed that his 1936 prediction wasn't a fluke: in the 20 presidential elections from 1936 to 2012, the final Gallup poll has predicted the winner 17 times—an 85 percent success rate. Not only has the Gallup poll almost always predicted the winner, it typically comes very close to predicting the popular vote margin. In those 20 elections, the final Gallup poll results have, on average, been within about 1.5 percent of the final election results.[1]

George Gallup pioneered scientific public opinion surveys, and the organization that bears his name has become an institution in the world of political polling. But these days, Gallup has plenty of competition. All four of the national newspapers in the United States regularly conduct political polls, each working with a polling partner: the *New York Times* and CBS News, the *Washington Post* and ABC News, the *Wall Street*

*Journal* and NBC News, and *USA Today* and Gallup. There are also a number of highly influential national polling organizations with no big-media affiliations, foremost of which are the Pew Research Center and Rasmussen Reports.

## HOW MODERN POLLING WORKS (AND WHY IT MATTERS)

Random sampling, the basic polling method George Gallup used over 75 years ago, is still the cornerstone of public opinion polling. Thanks to this method, all you need for a reasonably accurate view of *any* group, no matter how large, is about a thousand randomly selected people from that group. It probably seems hard to believe that so few people can accurately represent so many. It probably seems even harder to believe that the size of group you want to know about doesn't matter all that much. Want to accurately survey Cincinnati, Ohio? You'll need about a thousand people. A thousand will also do for a survey of the whole state of Ohio, or the entire United States, for that matter.

This is probability theory. To fully understand it, you'd need some statistical training, but if you're not exactly chomping at the bit to sign up for a statistics course, you can take my word for it: as long as people are *randomly* selected—which means that everybody in the group you're interested in (what statisticians call the population) has a roughly equal chance of being chosen—a survey of around a thousand people has about a 95 percent chance of getting within 3 to 4 percent of the "real" answer, that is, the answer you'd get if you talked to every single person in that population. That 3 to 4 percent is what's known of as the margin of error (which statisticians call the confidence interval), with the number smack in the middle of that margin—the number you'll usually see reported in the media—being the best estimation of the actual number.

If you don't want to take my word for it, you don't have to. Simply looking at the polls themselves is proof that the method works. Table 8.1 shows the final 2012 presidential poll results for all of the major media polls and the main independent polling organizations. The *least* accurate of them—Rasmussen and Gallup—missed by under 5 percent, and taken on average, the polls got to within 2.7 percent of the final popular vote margin. Over 128 million people voted for president in 2012, yet these fractionally small samples were able to come extremely close to the actual result.

While individual polls vary in their accuracy, aggregating multiple reputable polls almost always results in a final prediction that comes very close to what ends up happening. In the 2012 election, poll aggregator

**Table 8.1.   2012 Presidential Election Polls**

| Poll | Date Taken | Sample Size | Obama | Romney | Spread |
|------|-----------|-------------|-------|--------|--------|
| Gallup | 11/1–11/4 | 2,700 | 49 | 50 | Romney +1 |
| Pew Research | 10/31–11/3 | 2,709 | 50 | 47 | Obama +3 |
| Rasmussen | 11/3–11/5 | 1,500 | 48 | 49 | Romney +1 |
| CNN/Opinion Research | 11/2–11/4 | 693 | 49 | 49 | Tie |
| CBS/*NY Times* | 10/25–10/28 | 563 | 48 | 47 | Obama +1 |
| ABC/*Washington Post* | 11/1–11/4 | 2,345 | 50 | 47 | Obama +3 |
| NBC/*Wall Street Journal* | 11/1–11/3 | 1,475 | 48 | 47 | Obama +1 |
| **Poll Average** | | **1,712** | **48.9** | **48** | **Obama +0.9** |
| **Actual Results** | | **128 million** | **50.9** | **47.3** | **Obama +3.6** |

*Source:* Poll data from RealClearPolitics, accessed November 12, 2012, http://www.realclearpolitics.com/epolls/2012/president/us/general_election_romney_vs_obama-1171.html.

Nate Silver, who runs the *New York Times*'s *FiveThirtyEight* blog, became an instant celebrity (at least in the political geek world) thanks to his election predictions based on the results of nearly all available public polls. In the weeks before the election, Silver's massively aggregated poll model predicted that President Obama was an overwhelming favorite, much to the disbelief of many Romney supporters. Silver's final forecast—Obama 50.8, Romney 48.3—was nearly dead on, missing Romney's total by only 1 percent and getting to within 0.1 percent of Obama's vote.[2]

All reputable political polls use random selection and include a margin of error with their results. But that doesn't mean that media reports will mention the poll's margin of error. This becomes pretty important when a race is close: if you've got a 3 percent lead in a poll that has a 4 percent margin of error, you can't really say that you have a lead at all. Occasionally the media do comment on this, usually by saying that the race is a "statistical tie." But most of the time, that sort of language isn't used because the first thing people will probably think after hearing that a race is a statistical tie is, "What's a statistical tie?" At this point the media can either leave people confused or try to explain random sampling and margin of error, which in many cases will—leave people confused. Confusing your audience is rarely good for ratings.

Nearly all polls get their samples by using computers to randomly generate telephone exchange prefixes and numbers within those prefixes.

This works much better than using a telephone directory because it also brings in unlisted numbers (much to the annoyance of people who have unlisted numbers). And if you hope to avoid political survey calls by signing up on the national Do Not Call Registry, you're hoping in vain because when Congress passed the law in 2003 it made sure to exempt calls from organizations conducting political surveys. And despite what you might have heard on the Internet, survey organizations *can* legally call you on your cell phone, although they have to dial cell numbers by hand, which makes surveys that include cell phones more time-consuming and expensive: a national survey of about 1,500 people that includes cell phone users will run somewhere between $60,000 and $100,000.[3] Even telephone surveys that include cell phones don't reach everyone, but with 98 percent of American households having either a landline or cell service, it's close enough.[4] This hasn't always been the case—as late as the 1970s, over 10 percent of U.S. houses didn't have phone service, making telephone surveys less representative of the population than the traditional, and far more costly, house-to-house polls.[5]

## PROBLEMS WITH POLLS

Political scientist David Moore knows polls, both in theory and practice. After 20 years of teaching at the University of New Hampshire, Moore left academia and went to work for the Gallup Organization, where he eventually became managing editor of the Gallup poll. Here's what he has to say about political polling: "For years, we pollsters have systematically misled the American people about the accuracy of our polls, claiming a degree of precision in assessing public opinion that is far removed from reality."[6] Moore's view of polling seems to clearly contradict the evidence of the very accurate presidential election polls we've seen. To understand how both those polls *and* Moore can be right, we need to take a closer look at some of the biggest problems with political polls.

While polls overall are generally accurate, any individual poll might be considerably off the mark. Probability dictates that every once in a while, a random sample of people won't be representative of the whole. It's the same principle that tells us that if you flip a coin a thousand times, you'll almost always get around 500 heads and 500 tails, but every once in a while you'll end up with something more lopsided, like 700 heads and 300 tails. Earlier, I mentioned that a random sample of about a thousand people has around a 95 percent chance of getting to within 3 to 4 percent of the real answer, that is, the result you'd get if you talked to every single person in a population. Statisticians call this the poll's confidence level, and while 95 percent may seem like a pretty high level of confidence to have, it means that approximately 1 out of every 20 polls should come back with results that *aren't* within that plus or minus 3 percent margin of error. The media generally report on individual poll results, and so we usually can't tell how one specific poll compares to the findings of other polls. And because the media love to play up things that are new and exciting, poll results that differ from what's expected tend to get more coverage than findings that confirm what other polls have reported. Yet it would be a mistake to put too much faith in the findings of a single poll because of that 1-in-20 chance that it's not an accurate representation of the population as a whole.

This can be hard to spot most of the time because there generally just aren't enough poll results to compare. There are, however, some questions that multiple polling organizations ask all the time, one of which concerns whether or not people approve of the job the president is doing. If you looked at a plot of hundreds of presidential job approval polls taken over time—something you can find at the major poll aggregation sites—the first thing you'd notice would be a thick clustering of dots around the same area, which means that most of the polls conducted at the same time came up with very similar results. But if you looked a little closer you'd see the occasional dot that was set apart from the group—exactly what you would expect with a high (95 percent) but not perfect confidence level. Some polls just miss the mark. It's not the fault of the polling organization (usually)—it's simply how probability works.

The most important thing to remember is that although the media may make a big fuss over the latest poll, a smart media consumer knows that individual polls can sometimes be off, and it's always better to take a look at multiple polls on the same topic. This is virtually impossible to do if you're getting your poll data from TV, but thanks to poll aggregators like Real Clear Politics, the *Huffington Post*'s "Pollster," and Polling Report.com, it's easier than ever to step back from individual poll results and get a broader sense of what the public is thinking.

## ELECTION POLLS AND METEOROLOGY

Election polls are a lot like weather reports—the further out you go, the less accurate they are. You'll never see a weather forecast for a month from now because any responsible meteorologist knows that a prediction that far in the future would be little more than a guess. But we see plenty of far-out election predictions in the media, sometimes for elections that won't be held for years. And just like a weather report for next July, these early polls aren't anything you'd want to count on. Figure 8.1 shows end-of-month poll

**Figure 8.1.    Obama versus Romney Polling Averages**

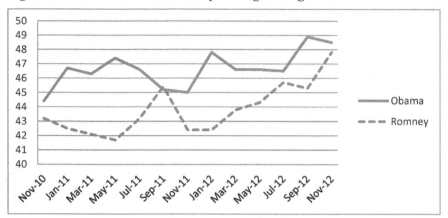

averages for nearly 600 presidential polls as compiled by the *Huffington Post*.[7] As you can clearly see, there were a number of ups and downs, with the polling averages rarely approaching the actual result.

Another thing to notice is that as the election approached the poll results started to converge, which makes perfect sense because more people make up their minds as the election draws near. Yet even in early polls, the vast majority of people *seem* to have picked a candidate. One big reason for this is that most polls ask people who they would vote for "if the election were held today." It's a question designed to force a choice even when the person answering it may have given the question virtually no consideration. When people tell pollsters that they're not sure who they'd vote for, it's common to ask the person to pick someone anyway—a practice you'd only know about if you dug deep into the guts of a polling report.

A good example of how forcing opinions can affect poll results comes from an August 2012 *Economist*/YouGov presidential preference poll. The main poll result reported by the media was that Obama was leading Romney by 3 points: 47 to 44 percent. (Three percent said they favored someone else, though that "other" preference typically isn't reported by the media.) On the face of it, the story this poll tells seems reasonably straightforward—months before the election, almost everyone has chosen a candidate, with Obama holding a slim lead over Romney. But buried in the polling report is this disclaimer: "Respondents who initially answered 'not sure' were then asked whom they would support if they had to choose. Those who answered 'Probably Obama' or 'Probably Romney' to the follow-up question are considered 'leaners' "[8] Without forcing the "not sure" people to make a choice, the result becomes Obama 43, Romney 41, and the number of undecided more than doubles, from 6 to 13 percent. Considering that the poll's margin of error was 4.2 percent (another important yet generally unreported fact) and you have what's essentially a toss-up, with plenty of people still undecided. But "Obama Up by 3" makes for a much snappier headline than "Too Close to Call Yet, Many Voters Unsure."

There are a number of things polling organizations *could* do to make their early election polls more meaningful. Simply asking people how likely they are to vote for someone instead of forcing a stark for-or-against choice would be a start. It would also be helpful if pollsters stopped asking people about who they would vote for if the election were held today and instead asked a nonhypothetical question along the lines of "Who do you think you will vote for on Election Day?"

One problem specific to national presidential polls is that the presidential election isn't really a national election. Thanks to the Electoral College system, it's actually a series of winner-take-all votes in each state,* meaning that a candidate can get more overall votes and lose the election. This may seem unlikely to you, but it's happened in 6.9 percent of all presidential elections,[†] most recently to Al Gore, who, in 2000, edged out George W. Bush in the popular vote by 0.5 percent but lost the electoral vote 271 to 266. What this means is that we would get a much better picture of how things truly stand in a presidential contest if we could look at 50 individual state polls instead of a single national poll. But 50 state polls, each of which would require drawing a sample of around 1,000 voters, are a lot more expensive to conduct than one national poll. It's also pretty difficult to summarize all those state polls and *then* explain the Electoral College, especially in a 30-second news segment. As far as most of the media is concerned, national polls are good enough, especially as most Americans will never know the difference. One of the main reasons so many pundits (particularly on the Republican side) believed the 2012 election was a toss-up was that they were focusing on the national polls, many of which had Obama and Romney running nearly even. But the preponderance of the evidence from the state polls showed that Romney was a long shot to win the presidency. In the days before the election, Nate Silver's *FiveThirtyEight* poll aggregator, which *did* examine multiple state polls, predicted Obama had a more than 90 percent chance of winning reelection, setting off howls of protest from Romney

---

*Except for Maine and Nebraska, which award one electoral vote for each congressional district, with two electoral votes going to the statewide winner.

[†]This has happened in 4 out of 58 elections. The percentage gives you more context than the number 4, unless you happened to know offhand that there have been 58 presidential elections. (In case you were really curious, it happened in the elections of 1824, 1876, 1888, and 2000.)

supporters who felt he couldn't possibly be right. But what Nate Silver knew was that in presidential elections, it's the state polls that really matter.*

National polls on who the major-party presidential nominees will be are even less worthwhile because party nominations are the result of state-level elections that take place over a six-month period. A lot can happen in six months, which is why presidential primary poll results often widely miss the mark. And yet many polling organizations begin asking voters about who their party's next nominee should be even before the new president is inaugurated. First out of the gate with a 2012 nominee poll was Rasmussen Reports, who polled Republicans on their choice for the 2012 GOP nomination *the day after* the 2008 presidential election. The prohibitive favorite was Sarah Palin, who was chosen by 64 percent of those surveyed. Mitt Romney, the eventual winner of the nomination, received only 11 percent in this insanely early poll.[9] Three months later CNN decided it was time for a poll of its own and found that Sarah Palin was still in the lead, but with only 29 percent, as opposed to the nearly two-thirds support she received in the Rasmussen poll.[10] And so it went for hundreds of national polls over nearly four years. The numbers would be almost meaningless for just about all of that time, but the news hole needs constant feeding, and the latest poll with fresh results was often just the thing to fill an empty slot.

In the end, all election polls can be measured against a clear standard: the result of the actual election. We can definitively say that Pew Research's final 2012 presidential poll (Obama 50, Romney 47) was more accurate than Rasmussen's final poll (Obama 48, Romney 49) because we know what happened on election day. But when people are polled on *issues* instead of candidates, there isn't any external accuracy check. Take, for instance, the issue of abortion. According to a Gallup poll taken in May of 2012, 25 percent of Americans believe abortion should be always legal. Barely more than two months later, a *Washington Post*/Kaiser Family Foundation survey found that only 19 percent of Americans believed abortion should always be legal. Not even a month after that, a CNN/Opinion Research poll found that 35 percent of Americans believed abortion should always be legal.[11] Did Americans' views on abortion—the most high-profile policy issue of the last

---

*Why didn't more Romney supporters realize this? Selective exposure and selective perception almost certainly played a big role. When the data pointed to a conclusion they didn't like, they either ignored it or found other, more comforting data on which to focus (like the national polls). Some Republicans knew Silver was probably right but didn't want to say so in the media for fear that it might depress Republican voter turnout, which could hurt nonpresidential GOP candidates.

40 years—seesaw that much over the course of a single summer? It seems highly unlikely. But if attitudes toward abortion are more stable than the dueling poll results would suggest, which poll comes closest to getting it right? Because we don't have national elections on abortion, or any other issue, there's no way to really know.

## POLITICIANS AND NATIONAL POLLS

Most of the polls we see in politics are national polls, which makes good financial sense for polling organizations and their media partners. The costs for surveying the entire country are roughly the same as for a state or local poll, but the national results are going to interest a lot more people. National polls can sometimes give us valuable information about the mood of the country as a whole, but in aggregating and averaging responses from all across one of the largest and most diverse countries in the world, national polls can gloss over an awful lot. Massachusetts and Mississippi are both part of the United States, but they're very different places, full of people with very different views of what the government should (and shouldn't) be doing.

This matters a lot in U.S. politics because we don't have national elections in this country. Presidents and senators are elected by the states, and members of the House of Representatives are chosen by districts within their states. And so a national poll showing that a majority of Americans favor gay marriage probably isn't going to mean much to a senator from Arkansas, where over three-quarters of the population is opposed to gay marriage.[12] This is also true for the presidency, which, as we've seen, may resemble a national election but is actually 50 statewide elections that happen on the same day. Because most states have a winner-take-all system of awarding their share of presidential electoral votes, a loss is a loss, whether it's by 100 votes or by 100,000 votes. This means that presidential candidates will pay much more attention to public opinion in the handful of "battleground" states that could go either way. Both Barack Obama and Mitt Romney would surely say that they cared just as much about Illinois (20 electoral votes) as they did about Ohio (18 electoral votes), but their travel schedules and campaign spending show that they lavished a lot more attention on battleground Ohio than they did on Obama's home state.

## FAKE OPINIONS

When we see poll results, we naturally tend to think that they're a reflection of what people are thinking. After all, that's the whole point of the process—someone wants to find out how the public feels about a candidate or an issue, so they ask a representative sample of the public, which gives them their answer. Except a lot of the time that's not actually how it works because plenty of people simply don't know or care enough to have meaningful opinions. There's no question that many Americans are woefully ignorant about politics, but when put on the spot and asked to give their opinion of a candidate or issue, plenty of them won't let ignorance stand in the way of speaking their mind. (We all know people like this.) According to a number of studies on public opinion, somewhere in the neighborhood of 30 percent of Americans are willing to give an opinion about an issue or program *that doesn't actually exist.*\*[13] If nearly a third of people are willing to make up an opinion about nothing, it's almost dead certain that plenty more are willing to offer opinions on real issues when they're essentially clueless.

Why would so many people make up opinions? Public opinion researchers say it has a lot to do with people not wanting to appear ignorant. Also, most people willing to take a survey really *do* want to be helpful. After years running the Gallup poll, David Moore concluded that, "people tend to be accommodating when they answer polls. If we pollsters want them to guess at an answer, they will."[14] If people guess at answers and make up opinions on the spot, regardless of whether it's to avoid looking dumb or to accommodate the pollster, the opinion that's being measured isn't a true reflection of public opinion.

Unfortunately, there's no simple way to know whether people responding to surveys have real or fake opinions. It's not impossible to check, but doing so would require longer and more involved surveys, something that would be even more off-putting to a public that isn't exactly crazy about surveys in the first place. And even if a polling organization did try to sort out real from fake opinions, the resulting poll would be a lot more difficult to present in the media. A typical polling story headline looks something like this: "New Poll Shows 60 Percent of Americans Favor <Whatever>." A headline that included poll respondents' level of knowledge would have to be more like this: "New Poll Shows 45 Percent of Well-Informed Americans—Approximately 20 Percent of Those Responding —Favor <Whatever>, while 60 Percent of Poorly Informed Americans—about 40 Percent of Those Responding—Approve of <Whatever>." If that's confusing to you (which I'm betting it is—I wrote it and it's kind of confusing

---

\*How can we know this? It involves researchers misleading people by asking them how they feel about, for instance, "the president's response to recent unrest in East Warzistan." The correct response is "East Warzistan? What's East Warzistan?" but plenty of people will say something like, "The president is doing a *horrible* job with East Warzistan!"

to me), think how confusing it would be to people who don't know as much as you do. Bewildering your audience like that is not a recipe for must-see TV.

The process of issue polling itself probably distorts our understanding of public opinion. To get people's opinions on an issue, pollsters often feed people information they may not have previously had. This is commonly done through what's called the "As you may know . . ." question. A fairly representative example is this question from a 2010 Gallup poll on the economy, which begins, "As you may know, one part of the tax agreement reached by President Obama and Republicans in Congress extends for all Americans the income tax cuts passed in 2001 and 2003 that were set to expire on Dec. 31."[15] Did the people being asked that questions *really* know all that? Certainly some of them did, but how many? Maybe it would have been a good idea to ask people if they really *did* know this in the first place instead of assuming they did. But that would mean asking an additional question (a "Did you know that . . . ?" question) and then having to report two sets of results: one for people who actually *did* know, and another for people who had no idea and so were essentially being asked to come up with an instant opinion based on Gallup's 32-word summary, which doesn't quite qualify as a full policy briefing. And then there's the problem of people saying that they did know that, when really they didn't. So what percentage of Americans actually know the stuff in "As you may know . . ." questions? We don't know.

The way poll questions are worded can also have a significant effect on the answers people give. In March 2012, an ABC News/*Washington Post* poll asked, "Do you think health insurance companies should or should not be required to cover the full cost of birth control for women?" A healthy majority of 61 percent said that insurance companies should be required to provide coverage. But a CBS News/*New York Times* poll conducted at just about the same time found that only 40 percent of people felt coverage should have to be provided.[16] A big part of the reason for this large discrepancy is probably related to the way the CBS/*New York Times* poll asked the question: "Do you think health insurance plans for all employers should have to cover the full cost of birth control for their female employees, or should employers be allowed to opt out of covering that based on religious or moral objections?" If you compare the two questions, you'll see a noticeable difference in emphasis. The ABC/*Washington Post* question focuses on costs to health insurance companies. Lots of people don't like health insurance companies, which probably contributed to the high percentage of "should" responses. By contrast, the CBS/*New York Times* question puts the emphasis not on insurance companies but on employers, making it a question about whether they should have the freedom to "opt out for religious or moral reasons." Although question wording can have a significant effect on how people answer, the media will almost never feature the actual wording of poll questions when reporting on the latest public opinion findings.

The order in which questions are asked can also have an effect on the answers given, with earlier questions providing context that can influence later answers. The Pew Research Center, in its primer on question order effects, gives the example of a poll it conducted in 2008. One of the questions concerned satisfaction with how things were going in the country, while another inquired about people's approval or disapproval of then-President Bush. When the satisfaction question was asked first, 17 percent said they were satisfied and 25 percent reported approval of President Bush. When the question order was flipped, approval of President Bush stayed about the same (24 percent) but satisfaction dropped all the way down to 9 percent.[17] Question order can matter a lot, but there's no simple way for the media to report on it—just like with question wording, if you want to know, you're forced to find the original survey questions and look through them yourself. Almost nobody is going to do that, and so the ways in which question order distorts public opinion are going to be almost entirely hidden from us.

## INTENSITY MATTERS

I'm from Cleveland, and so I like the Cleveland Cavaliers. But I *love* the Pittsburgh Steelers. It's a difference that really matters in my everyday life (sad but true). For example, I don't have any Cavaliers merchandise, but I've bought crates of Steelers gear. If I moved to, say, Detroit, it's possible I could become a Pistons fan, but there's absolutely no way I could ever abandon the Steelers for the Lions. I know this to be true in my very bones. It may sound silly, but if you're a sports fan, you know exactly what I mean.

This isn't just a sports thing—it applies just as well to politics, and it matters for all the same reasons. The more strongly you feel about an issue or a candidate, the more probable it is that you'll be an active supporter. Of the millions of people who like Mitt Romney, it's not the ones who felt he was "okay, I guess" that sent him money and volunteered for his campaign. It's the people who thought he was ultra-super-awesome who did all that. And the "okay, I guess" people are going to be a lot more willing to abandon their lukewarm allegiance and get on with their lives than are those die-hards who dreamed sweet Romney dreams at night. Yet most polls don't even ask people about how strongly they feel, and if they do, it's rarely reported in the media. There are two basic reasons for this. The first is that asking people how strongly they feel means keeping them on the phone longer, and the longer you're on the phone, the more likely you are to hang up. Hang-ups are bad for business. The second reason is that reporting intensity along with opinion is harder than just reporting opinion alone, which is why even when there is intensity data available, the media generally choose to ignore it.

Ignoring opinion intensity can sometimes have major consequences. For example, just before the U.S. invasion of Iraq in 2003, a CNN/*USA Today*/Gallup poll found that 59 percent of Americans favored war, with only 38 percent in opposition. A number of other polls taken during the same period came up with support levels as high or higher, seemingly indicating solid public backing for war. While most polling organizations asked only the simple "do you support or oppose" question, Gallup tried something different by including a follow-up question that asked people whether they would be upset if the United States went against their preference. Only 29 percent of those who supported military action said they'd be upset if the United States didn't go to war, with 30 percent of antiwar people saying they'd be upset if the United States invaded. People who weren't sure if they'd be upset or not were the largest group, comprising 41 percent of respondents.[18] This makes what seemed like fairly strong public support for war—support that, by many accounts, played an important role in the decision to eventually invade Iraq—look a lot weaker. Maybe intensity-based polling wouldn't have changed the eventual decision, but considering how big of a decision it was, a few more polling organizations might have at least asked.

## WHAT TO LOOK FOR IN A POLL

When you see a poll report, the first question you should ask yourself is "Whose poll is it?" You can pretty safely assume that polls conducted by major media organizations or well-respected national polling groups like Gallup or the Pew Center are professionally designed and administered and follow all the basic guidelines for scientific polling. Polls that come from sources you haven't heard of may not be all that professional—don't be quite as quick to trust them, especially if they report results different from those of well-known and respected polling organizations.

The second important question to ask is, "What's the margin of error?" If a poll's margin of error is larger than the percentage difference between two candidates or positions, you can't say with any confidence that one has greater support than another. Finding the margin of error will usually require looking past the headlines, but the print media at least generally does a good job of providing that information in their presentation of survey results. TV news doesn't do nearly as well, and even when a reporter does mention a poll's margin of error, it's usually done very quickly in a few seconds at the end of the piece. If you're not listening closely, it's easy to miss.

Finding out who conducted a poll and checking the margin of error are simple things that take almost no time. Doing these things will put you way ahead of most people, but no matter how much you know about any single poll it's important to remember that because of how random sampling works, there's a small but not insignificant chance that any single poll won't be representative of the population. And so if you're able, it's a really good idea to look at a bunch of polls taken around the same time: if they're all coming up with similar results, you can have a lot more confidence in what's being reported. Most major political news sources won't report multiple polls, or won't do it very prominently, because they're pushing their own poll results and don't want to promote their competition. But thanks to online poll aggregator sites it's not too difficult to examine a bunch of polls on many important races and issues. It will only take a few minutes, and as a result you'll have a much better sense of public opinion (which will put you further ahead of most everyone else).

If you'd like an even better understanding of what poll results mean, take a look at how the questions were worded. Sometimes the full wording of a question is included with the news story accompanying it, in which case it's pretty simple to check out. But often you're given a highly abbreviated version of the question, one that doesn't give you a real sense of what people were actually responding to. If you're getting your news online, there may be a link to the complete question list, allowing you to see the actual wording for yourself. But if your news is coming from a nononline source, you're pretty much out of luck. If you do end up pulling up a question list, you might also want to check the order in which questions were asked and think about how that might have influenced the results.

Even if you don't do any of these things, you can still be a much smarter than average consumer of political polls by simply remembering that while polls can be useful, they're not the precise measures of public opinion their creators would like you to believe they are. Much of the public opinion you're exposed to is manufactured by media companies that are far more interested in getting your attention than they are in giving you a clear picture of what people are really thinking about politics.

## NOTES

1. "Election Polls—Accuracy Record in Presidential Elections," Gallup, http://www.gallup.com/poll/9442/Election-Polls-Accuracy-Record-Presidential -Elections.aspx, and "Romney 49%, Obama 48% in Gallup's Final Election Survey," Gallup, http://www.gallup.com/poll/158519/romney-obama-gallup -final-election-survey.aspx, both accessed December 21, 2012.

2. Nate Silver, "Nov. 5: Late Poll Gains for Obama Leave Romney with Longer Odds," *FiveThirtyEight*, November 6, 2012, http://fivethirtyeight.blogs .nytimes.com/2012/11/06/nov-5-late-poll-gains-for-obama-leave-romney-with -longer-odds/.

3. Robert J. Samuelson, "Pollsters' Moment of Truth," *Washington Post*, October 29, 2012, http://www.washingtonpost.com/opinions/robert-j-samuelson -pollsters-moment-of-truth/2012/10/28/5c4f5a38-211c-11e2-ac85-e669876c6a24 _story.html?tid=wp_ipad.

4. Stephen J. Blumberg and Julian V. Luke, "Wireless Substitution: Early Release of Estimates from the National Health Interview Survey, January– June 2010," Centers for Disease Control and Prevention, accessed December 21, 2012, http://www.cdc.gov/nchs/data/nhis/earlyrelease/wireless201012.htm#table3.

5. "Historical Census of Housing Tables—Telephones," Census Bureau, accessed July 7, 2012, http://www.census.gov/hhes/www/housing/census/historic/ phone.html.

6. David W. Moore, *The Opinion Makers: An Insider Exposes the Truth behind the Polls* (Boston: Beacon Press, 2009), xiv.

7. "2012 General Election: Romney vs. Obama," *Huffington Post*, accessed January 3, 2013, http://elections.huffingtonpost.com/pollster/2012-general -election-romney-vs-obama.

8. "The Economist. YouGov Poll," accessed December 21, 2012, http://cdn .yougov.com/cumulus_uploads/document/lfu8cg1oh5/econToplines.pdf.

9. "Toplines—GOP—November 5, 2008," Rasmussen Reports, accessed December 21, 2012, http://www.rasmussenreports.com/public_content/politics/ questions/pt_survey_questions/november_2008/toplines_gop_november_5_2008.

10. Paul Steinhauser, "Poll: GOP Split over Possible 2012 Contenders," CNN, February 27, 2009, http://www.cnn.com/2009/POLITICS/02/27/gop.poll/.

11. "Abortion and Birth Control," PollingReport.com, accessed August 26, 2012, http://www.pollingreport.com/abortion.htm.

12. "2011 Arkansas Poll Summary Report.pdf," accessed December 21, 2012, http://www.uark.edu/depts/plscinfo/partners/arkpoll/11/2011% 20Arkansas%20Poll%20summary%20report.pdf.

13. Norbert Schwarz, *Cognition and Communication: Judgmental Biases, Research Methods, and the Logic of Conversation* (Mahwah, NJ: Psychology Press, 1996).

14. Moore, *The Opinion Makers*, 23.

15. "Taxes," Gallup, accessed December 21, 2012, http://www.gallup.com/poll/1714/taxes.aspx#2.

16. "Abortion and Birth Control," PollingReport.com, accessed August 26, 2012, http://www.pollingreport.com/abortion.htm.

17. "Question Order," Pew Research Center, accessed December 21, 2012, http://www.people-press.org/methodology/questionnaire-design/question-order/.

18. Moore, *The Opinion Makers*, 6–7.

# NINE

## What's in Your Cognitive Toolkit?

### INTRODUCTION

If you've gotten this far, you already know some pretty important things: why political news is the way it is, how bias and irrationality affect the news we get and how we interpret it, and the many ways that numbers can be manipulated to paint an incomplete and sometimes downright misleading picture of political reality. Awareness of these things should, by itself, make you a smarter political news consumer. But considering all the biased political information in the media, as well as our natural tendencies toward irrationality, we often need more than just awareness. Now that you have a basic blueprint for how political media work, you need some tools to construct a more rational and better-informed political media environment for yourself.

This chapter will look at a number of tools that can be useful as you try to make sense of the political world. Not every tool is appropriate for every job, but with a little bit of judicious consideration on your part, you should be able to find a few that work for you, whatever your situation may be. Ernest Hemingway once said, "Every man should have a built-in automatic crap detector operating inside him." With any luck, what you'll learn in this chapter will help you construct (or improve) your very own automatic political crap detector.

### CONSIDER THE SOURCE

One of the most important things you can do is to look into where the evidence supporting various political claims and arguments comes from.

Reputable political news generally includes information about sources. Online news can be particularly useful here because online news stories often include direct links to source material, whether it's as hyperlinks in the story itself, part of a sidebar feature, or at the end of the article. Even when direct links aren't included—which, obviously, is the case for all non-online news—sources are almost always mentioned somewhere in the story. With this basic information, it often only takes a quick Google search to check the evidence for yourself. If you're serious about a particular issue, checking the facts is really important. As former *New York Times* Washington bureau chief Bill Kovach says, "When everything is unchecked, all assertions become equal—those that are accurate and those that are not. The news, in journalism, becomes more of an argument than the depiction of accurate events that argument, debate, and compromise can build upon."[1]

The big problem here is that nobody (including me) does all that much checking. Fact-checking political news is almost nobody's idea of Big Fun, and even if you do happen to find it oddly enjoyable, it would just take too long to do for every story. Even those of us who do a bit of digging into sources tend to be very selective about what we check, generally not bothering to confirm evidence that matches our preexisting beliefs and only looking further when a truly surprising claim is being made. Although it's easier than ever to check sources, thanks to online links as well as fact-checking sites like Politifact.com and Factcheck.org, we still almost never bother. That's not going to change, and so telling you to check your sources is like reminding you to brush after every meal: good advice that you'll ignore more often than not because you're got too much other stuff to do.

Even though you won't generally go to all the trouble to actually check sources, there are a few simple things you can do to help determine the quality of the evidence you're being given. The most basic thing is to simply notice if there are any links or clear references to sources. You don't have to actually check them out—but if you don't find any you should be at least a little bit suspicious. Sometimes this information isn't included due to space or time considerations, but not clearly mentioning or linking to a source might also be a sign of sloppy reporting or a bad political argument. That's not to say that stories that link to source materials are always correctly reporting on or interpreting their sources (they're not), but other things being equal, you can place a bit more trust in political news and commentary that clearly reveals its sources.

As an example of how you might do this, let's take look at an article by Paul Krugman, one of the most influential political columnists in the United States. In his *New York Times* column of June 7, 2012, Krugman argued that President Reagan, a hero to many fiscal conservatives, was actually a bigger spender than President Obama has proven to be.[2] To support this, Krugman writes that at the same point in their presidencies, government spending had gone up by 14.4 percent under Reagan, while it increased by only 6.4 percent under Obama. Krugman doesn't cite a source for this data, which should send up a warning right away. However, a quick click on Krugman's biography link will tell you that he's an economist with degrees from Yale and MIT and that he received the Nobel Prize in Economics in 2008. Based on this, as well as knowing that he's writing for the most influential political news outlet in the United States, you might feel comfortable assuming that he's not just making up these numbers. But his biography page also tells us that he writes a blog called *The Conscience of a Liberal*. Also, we know that the *New York Times* has a reputation for having a liberal op-ed section. So based on this additional information, it seems reasonable to think Paul Krugman might be inclined to emphasize the numbers in a way that would make President Obama look good.* This simple checking took under a minute, and it gave us some pretty useful context for evaluating Krugman's claims about the economy.

Another useful fact-checking shortcut is to learn a few basic things about the organization that created the information. Much of the evidence behind political arguments comes from government agencies or major national polling organizations, which are typically trustworthy. But you're also likely to find a lot of evidence and arguments coming from political think tanks, which are private organizations that research and analyze politics, typically in order to advance a certain agenda. Some of the most commonly cited think tanks, such as the Kaiser Family Foundation or the Council on Foreign Relations, aren't ideologically motivated, while others, like the Heritage Foundation (conservative) and the Economic Policy Institute (EPI; liberal) most definitely take sides.[3] Sometimes, the media will indicate whether a think tank is ideologically biased, but that's not always the case, even in the same newspaper. For example, in an article on April 9, 2012, the *New York Times* refers to the EPI as "a left-leaning research organization,"[4] but in an article the *Times* published only a few months later, EPI is identified as "a research group in Washington that studies the labor market."[5] Both of these descriptions are accurate, but only the first tells you that the group might be consistently presenting and interpreting evidence that favors liberal interests.

---

*Which he sort of admits by stating, later in the article, that his numbers include *all* government spending, including spending by state and local governments—spending that neither President Reagan nor President Obama had control over. But although he mentions this, Krugman doesn't present the data on federal spending alone, which would be a much better comparison of the two presidents.

As a general rule, the further away you get from the mainstream media, the more skeptical you should be about the evidence you're presented with. Big media organizations have the resources to hire top reporters, editors, and support staff; something that most smaller organizations simply can't afford. That's why most of the political news you see was initially reported on by the mainstream media. Political commentary is a lot less expensive than original reporting, which is why it's much more common in the nonmainstream media. Commentators earn their living by being "interesting," which means that they're a lot more likely to use questionable sources, not disclose the political leanings of their sources, and neglect to mention important (but inconvenient) information. This is true regardless of where the political commentary appears, but there's more of it in smaller political news outlets, and it's probably not scrutinized as closely as it would be if it appeared in a national newspaper or network broadcast.

## TANSTAAFL

TANSTAAFL, a long and awkward acronym that is a favorite of economists, points to an important truth about politics that you should always keep in mind when getting your news: "There ain't no such thing as a free lunch." This phrase, which was coined by libertarian science fiction writer Robert Heinlein, became so well-known in economics circles that Nobel Prize–winning economist Milton Friedman used it as the title for his 1975 book. It means that you can't get something for nothing because there are inevitable tradeoffs in every choice you make—something that is true both for politics and life in general. Nearly everyone understands this on one level: if we want new roads, we have to find the money to pay for them; a big tax break means less money for the government, which in turn means either more borrowing or cuts in government programs (or some combination of the two). What we're less likely to consider is that every choice we make also imposes what economists call an opportunity cost, meaning that by making *any* choice (including no choice at all) we forgo the opportunity to do everything but what we've chosen at that point in time. For instance, if President Obama decides to spend 15 minutes talking about foreign policy, he can't spend that same 15 minutes talking about the economy. As media consumers, we're constantly faced with opportunity costs: if you have half an hour to catch the news, spending it reading the *Wall Street Journal* means you'll miss out on what the *Washington Post* and Fox News have to say.

The reason that TANSTAAFL should be an important part of your cognitive toolkit is that it's so basic that it can easily fade into the background.

The media has no interest in bringing it up, as it's hard to imagine anything that could be more dull than a constant reminder that every choice we make closes off other choices. Whenever you hear about what a politician plans to do for (or to) you, it's useful to ask two basic TANSTAAFL questions: "What do we have to give up to get that?" and "What else could we do with the time we'd have to spend on it?" Most people with more than a passing interest in politics will consider the first of these questions right away. It's the second one that's often forgotten.

During his first year in office, President Obama spent a great deal of time and effort pushing through the Affordable Care Act (a.k.a. Obama-care), a major change to the nation's health care system. During that time, anyone with even a passing interest in U.S. politics heard endless cover-age of the political maneuverings and policy implications of the plan and was exposed ("subjected" might be a better word) to a multitude of analy-ses from all sides about what the plan would cost, who it would benefit, and how it would be paid for. What most of the media—and most citizens—ignored was what Republicans and Democrats could be doing *instead of* debating health care reform. The silence on this wasn't complete—all along there were people who argued that by spending so much time on health care, President Obama was neglecting the economy—but for the most part, all those health care stories focused on health care itself and not all the issues that health care was pushing to the sidelines.

The same was true for the biggest thing President Obama's predecessor did. In the lead-up to the war in Iraq, the press was focused mainly on the justifications for the war and the domestic and international support for the Bush administration's push to invade. The question of whether spend-ing all this time on Iraq was causing the United States to lose focus on the war in Afghanistan was out there, but unless you were paying close atten-tion you would have been unlikely to hear much about this particular opportunity cost (though after the fighting had stopped in Iraq and the sit-uation in Afghanistan seemed to be deteriorating, the question began to be raised more prominently). The lack of focus on opportunity costs can be seen even in the public opinion polling that was being done at the time: none of the major polling organizations even asked questions about the opportunity costs of either health care reform or the war in Iraq. That makes perfect sense from the media's standpoint because covering things that people *aren't* talking about isn't a particularly good way to attract an audience. Unfortunately, just because an issue isn't being talked about doesn't mean it isn't important.

## FALSIFIABILITY

Karl Popper, generally considered one of the greatest modern philosophers of science, made many important contributions to our understanding of how we come to know things. One of his key insights involved what he called *falsifiability*—the idea that the true test of a scientific theory is whether or not it can be potentially proven false. If you can't think of a way your theory could be wrong, it's not a scientific theory: it's an unscientific belief. Popper's point applies equally well to political views, which makes it a good way to examine what we believe about politics. That's because, as we've already seen, we almost always choose and interpret our political media in a way that reinforces our preexisting beliefs. Simply asking yourself the question, "What would it take for me to conclude I'm wrong about this?" helps to remind you that it's possible for you to be mistaken, something that's all too easy for us to conveniently forget, especially when it comes to those political views we feel most passionately attached to. If you're willing to take a shot at actually answering that question, you'll probably find it difficult because doing so requires you to essentially argue against yourself, even though that argument is built on hypothetical evidence. The best most people can do is to put together some sad little straw man of a counterargument, which they then see as confirming their belief that they were right in the first place. And maybe they (meaning you—and me) actually *are* right, but what's almost certainly going on is a negative reaction to cognitive dissonance, which makes even *considering* circumstances under which you may not be right an unpleasant chore.

And so you shouldn't think of this simple exercise as trying to prove yourself wrong because unless you're an extraordinarily open-minded person, you'll almost never succeed. When people change their political views, it rarely happens in a blinding flash of insight. How it usually works is that evidence slowly builds up over time, with the actual change often being nearly imperceptible. But if you close yourself off to even the *possibility* that you might be mistaken, it's going to be a lot harder for contrary evidence to take root. Regularly asking yourself how you might be wrong helps you to keep you receptive to new information and gives you room to grow and change politically.

It's also helpful to use this question in reverse by asking yourself how it might be possible that a political view you disagree with could be correct. Let's say you believe that global climate change is real, that it is caused by human activities, and that government has a responsibility to take steps to minimize any present or future environmental damage it results in. If you hear someone on TV saying "climate change is a hoax," you'll probably immediately dismiss this person as stupid, naïve, or just plain bad (possibly some combination of all three). That initial reaction is going to come pretty quickly, and there's not a whole lot you can do about it. It's also probably expecting too much for you to think, "Maybe this person is right, and I'm wrong." A more reasonable approach is to ask yourself, "What evidence would I need in order to agree with this person?"* Again, even though you're unlikely to take the time to fully answer this question, just asking it should help to keep your mind a little bit more open and reinforce to you the importance of good information in forming political views. This is no quick and simple solution, but if you practice it on a regular basis, you're likely to find yourself at least a little bit more politically flexible and open to new ideas.

## BEWARE LINEAR EXTRAPOLATION

Linear extrapolation is a geeky way to describe our tendency to assume that things will keep on going the way they've been going. This can be very useful in dealing with a relatively simple environment over a short time period: if you see a car careening toward you, the smart thing to do is to assume that it's going to keep on coming (and get out of the way). But because the political environment is almost always incredibly complex and changes a great deal over time, this tendency can frequently steer us wrong. The media love to make projections about the future of this or that policy, and quite naturally those predictions are based on current information, which is all we really have to go on. Over short periods this can work out reasonably well, but the further out the prediction is, the more likely things are to change.

One of many examples of this involves oil—always a big political issue. For decades, American politicians have been worrying about our dependence on imported oil, often pointing to research from the highly regarded U.S. Geological Survey (USGS) concerning exactly how much oil we have left. In 1995, the USGS reported that the United States had 151 million barrels of recoverable oil—not all that much considering that in the same year we used 17.7 million barrels of oil.[6] But it turns out that this figure was not just off but *way* off. In 2008, the USGS announced that there were between

---

*Some conservatives argue that climate change isn't even a real scientific theory because it fails Popper's falsifiability test—*any* current weather condition you can think of can be (and has been) attributed to climate change. Supporters of climate change theory will say that's because weather isn't climate, which is weather over a long period of time.

3.0 and 4.3 *billion* barrels of recoverable oil—not in the United States as a whole, but in just in a single area covering North Dakota and Montana.[7] While nobody could have possibly known that the earlier oil reserve estimates would be so far off, the media should have realized that technology improves and estimates can change and reflected that uncertainty in their reporting instead of treating long-range estimates as unalterable reality.

This sort of thing happens all the time in budget forecasting. The federal budget is a huge and massively complex thing, meaning that predictions concerning what it will look like in the distant future are extremely speculative. Yet this doesn't prevent the media and politicians from speculating away. In 1999, after nearly a decade of peace and prosperity, predictions of budget surpluses as far as the eye can see abounded in the media. In November of that year, *Fortune* magazine declared, "The time couldn't be riper for a tax cut. The federal budget surplus is expected to total $3 trillion over the next decade, and both political parties are clamoring to reduce taxes."[8] Taxes ended up being cut, but the prediction of $3 trillion in surplus was ludicrously wrong. It took only three years for the budget to go back into the red. By the end of a decade that was predicted to end with a $3 trillion surplus, the federal government had racked up over $3.4 trillion in debt, thanks to a major war and the worst economic downturn since the Great Depression.[9] A forecast that's off by more than $6 trillion dollars hardly inspires confidence. And yet year after year, long-term predictions just like this are made, with scant acknowledgement that they're often little better than guesswork. Big, complex systems are inherently hard to predict—just try to get an accurate weather forecast for a month from now. This isn't usually the fault of the people doing the predicting; in fact, in most cases the predictions that are highlighted by the media and politicians come with a boatload of qualifiers that never make the news. For example, the Congressional Budget Office (CBO), a nonpartisan agency that's the source of many budget forecasts, works on the assumption that every law currently in place will stay in place without any changes. That's a completely unrealistic assumption, but as the CBO itself points out, "There is no plausible alternative to that approach."[10] In other words, we have a choice between long-term budget forecasts based on unrealistic assumptions, or no long-term budget forecasts at all. The CBO is the most capable budget forecasting organization in all of U.S. politics, and even it misses wildly all the time. In 2004, the CBO estimated that a recently enacted Medicare drug program would cost $348 billion between 2006 and 2010. The actual cost ended up being $149 billion less. That's because the CBO guesstimated that 42.1 million people would enroll in the program, when only 10.6 million actually did.[11] That's not just missing—that's missing by a mile.

Forecasts tend to be the least accurate when they try to predict the effect of big new programs. As former CBO Director Douglas Elmendorf noted, "When Congress is considering incremental changes to policies, and especially incremental changes that are similar to ones that have been made before, then there's a history that we and other analysts can consult [but with] more dramatic or novel changes in policy, there's no previous experience to refer to."[12] There's no sense in blaming the CBO or any other forecasting agency—long-range political forecasts are always going to be tenuous at best. So when you hear confident-sounding political predictions that go out any further than a few years, be very skeptical because things change, and nobody can predict everything that's coming around the corner.

## SOME OTHER USEFUL TOOLS

The four cognitive tools mentioned above are great for general-purpose use, and once you start working with them, you'll find they can apply to almost all the political news you come in contact with. To round out your cognitive toolkit, you might also find a few reminders useful. One of them has to do with something you probably don't realize you have: chronic apophenia. Although it sounds like some unfortunate medical condition, it's actually your natural tendency to impose patterns on things that are more or less random. Evolution has designed humans to be pattern recognizers that can quickly figure out what causes what and how things go together. We're pretty amazing at doing this with visual data and simple logic puzzles, but the same wiring that makes us great at figuring out where Waldo is also leaves us vulnerable to seeing patterns that may not exist. That opens us up to the post hoc fallacy and also to all sorts of other bad arguments, most notably hasty generalization, argument by innuendo, false analogy, and proof by verbosity. Whenever you find yourself seeing a pattern in politics, it's good to remind yourself that you're designed to find patterns even when there aren't any patterns to be found.

Another inherent tendency we have is to exaggerate the importance of things that are happening right now, something psychologists call the focusing illusion. This is another natural human trait that made a lot of sense when paying extremely close attention to our environment could mean the difference between eating or being eaten. Politics rarely involves those sort of instantaneous big choices, but we can't just switch off a few hundred thousand years of evolution when we turn on MSNBC. The best we can do is to keep in mind that regardless of what the story (or scandal) of the day is, it's rarely as big of a deal as we think it is. Along the same lines, it also helps to keep in mind that the news media goes to great lengths to play up the importance of political developments because it's a lot harder to grab your attention with news that isn't really all that important. Today's earth-shattering development is probably going to be almost entirely forgotten next month (or next week). Instead of letting yourself get caught up in the largely pointless frenzy, try to remind yourself that you (and the media) are prone to overreact.

## RED FLAGS

In addition to using these cognitive tools, you should also be on the lookout for red flags—words or phrases that should immediately put your political crap detector on high alert. One of the most commonly used red flag phrases is the "simple" or "common-sense" solution to the political problem of the day. It's almost always used by someone trying to convince you that things aren't really as complex as the other side wants you to believe, and if "they" would simply use their common sense, the problem could be easily solved. Obviously, the other side either has no common sense or is being irrationally obstructionist. Whatever the case, they're clearly not fit to govern. Examples of this red flag are thick on the ground: a Google News search for the phrase "common-sense solution" turns up hundreds of results, including common-sense solutions for everything from public access to local hiking paths[13] to fixing the federal budget,[14] most of which also have the virtue of being simple or easy solutions (sometimes both). Both Democrats and Republicans routinely present "common-sense" solutions, though as you might expect, what seems like common sense to one party generally strikes the other side as being a really bad idea.

Calls for common-sense solutions tap into our desire to believe that the political world isn't as complex as it sometimes appears and that there are always clearly definable ways to make things right (or at least better). Unfortunately, many of the common-sense solutions for political problems are similar to the familiar common-sense solution for losing weight—eat less calorie-dense, highly processed junk and exercise more. For millions of Americans it's not that simple. They'll point out that it's hard to find time to exercise regularly, or that processed foods are so much more convenient, or that healthy foods spoil (which isn't a problem with Hungry Man Dinners). Plus, the kids just hate vegetables. So although the solution to this problem is both common-sense and simple, there are a huge number of things making it really difficult to implement. Most of us understand this when it comes to something like weight loss, yet we're often unwilling to accept that the same reasoning might apply to national political issues, which are almost certainly a whole lot more complicated than your epic struggle to take off that last 10 pounds. It's a very safe bet that if someone's telling you there's a common-sense or simple solution for the political problem du jour, you're not being told the whole story. And if you find yourself thinking in terms of common-sense, simple political solutions, you should definitely take a closer look at your reasoning.

Another big red flag is the use of absolutes and unconditionals in political arguments. As much as some of us would like to believe it, most things in politics aren't black or white—almost everything in politics is some shade of gray. Has President Obama blamed President Bush for the economy? Absolutely. Does he *always* blame President Bush? Of course not. But that *always* just feels so much more lively than something like, "President Obama has, on occasion, been known to blame President Bush." Precision can be awfully dull, and dull stories don't sell.

Another popular red flag is the "scheme." If you see this word in reference to anyone or anything in politics, you can be just about certain that the person doing the talking or writing is against it. Not too many people are eager to be associated with a scheme. "Plans," "programs," and even "strategies" are okay, but you'll seldom hear anyone in politics say, "Let me tell you about this new scheme I've come up with." It just sounds shady. But schemes are attributed to politicians all the time. President Obama has "schemes" for energy, jobs, patient dumping (that one wouldn't even sound good as a "program"), and taxes, to name just a few. He seems to be quite the schemer, but his predecessor in the White House more than held his own with assorted war schemes, his bailout scheme, his tax scheme (tax schemes are big favorites—every serious politician has to have them), and his energy scheme. When you see or hear "scheme," assume the person using it is trying to manipulate you.

"Risky" and "extreme" are also common red-flag words you should be on the lookout for. At the very least, they let you know that you're being warned away from someone or something—nobody gets people to support their candidate by saying, "Check this guy out—he's risky and extreme!" Every once in a while you might even run across the red-flag trifecta: a "risky, extreme scheme," an almost certain indicator that reasoned argument has been entirely abandoned in favor of emotional invective.

Then there are the "wars" that aren't actually wars. This dates back to at least President Lyndon Johnson's "War on Poverty" in the 1960s (update: poverty is still holding its own). More recently, in addition to the *actual* war in Afghanistan (the one most people sort of forgot about because it got kind of boring after the first decade), President Obama has waged all sorts of other wars. "To stop the war on American jobs we must end Obama's war on coal,"[15] blared Fox News in a recent headline. But that's only scratching the surface—the liberal website Mother Jones has compiled a list of 109 "wars" declared by President Obama, which range from the predictable—his wars on banks, unborn babies, and Fox News—to the more esoteric (Cheerios, vegan shops, and the Bowl Championship Series).[16] Obama's predecessor, George W. Bush was also no slacker when it came to wars. In addition to the real wars in Iraq and Afghanistan, and the not-technically-a-war on terror, President Bush somehow found time to declare war on the Bill of Rights,[17] women,[18] and even science.[19] "Class warfare" is a favorite of both Democrats and Republicans because it's so flexible: Democrats can cry "class warfare" whenever a Republican proposes to cut a social spending program, and Republicans can turn around and claim the same thing when a Democrats suggests higher taxes for top earners. If someone's calling it a war and there's no actual shooting going on, they're trying to appeal to your emotions over your reason.

Another favorite tactic of politicians and political pundits is to call their opponents elitists or part of the political elite. It's a fairly ridiculous claim to make in most cases because almost everyone running for high political office is part of the social and economic elite. This is especially true of presidential candidates: both Barack Obama and Mitt Romney have graduate degrees from Harvard (Romney's got *two* Harvard degrees—an MBA and a law degree). George W. Bush was a Harvard MBA, and John Kerry, his 2004 opponent, got his bachelor's degree from Yale. Chances are good that if you're running the country, or if you're in a position to do so, you're an elite (whether you're willing to admit it or not).

"Elitist" is often accompanied by another red flag term: "out of touch," as in "Obama (or Romney—take your pick) is an out-of-touch elitist" The idea is to suggest that the person in question doesn't understand what "regular people" or "real Americans" (two other phrases to be suspicious of) have to deal with. In one sense this is probably true—people who are part of the economic and political elite live very different lives from the rest of us, and it's highly unlikely that they can fully appreciate what life is like for the majority of us nonelite Americans. This plays right into our tendency toward groupism—if we see a candidate as fundamentally different from us, it makes it easier to dislike them. The phrases "elite" and "out of touch" encourage us to believe that anyone who hasn't shared our experiences can't be fully trusted.

But just because a politician has never worked on a factory floor or doesn't know how much a gallon of gas costs doesn't mean that he can't understand the macroeconomic consequences of the loss of manufacturing jobs or how energy price increases effect disposable household income. In fact, most "out of touch political elites" probably have a considerably better understanding of these things than people who work in "real jobs" and fill up their tanks with regular unleaded every week. So the next time you hear some politician being dismissed as an out of touch elite, instead of replying "That's awful!" you might want to say, "Well, I sure hope so!"

## LESS IS (OFTEN) MORE

You might think that half a dozen cognitive tools and a relatively short list of red flags to look out for couldn't possibly cover every situation you'll face as a consumer of political news. If so, you'd be right: there are a lot of other good cognitive tools and techniques out there. If you're interested in learning about more of them, you'll find all sorts of potentially useful stuff in the many books that have been written on critical thinking or improving your thinking. Most of these books are mind-numbingly dull, but there are a few that won't immediately put you to sleep. (One of the best recent books in this area is Edge.org's *This Will Make You Smarter: New Scientific Concepts to Improve Your Thinking*.)

But the fuller your cognitive toolbox gets, the harder it can be to remember what's in there. That's why I've kept it (relatively) short and simple, focusing only on those things that come up again and again in political news. Expanding your collection of cognitive tools can be a very good thing to do, but it's best to first become comfortable using some basics and go from there.

## NOTES

1. Bill Kovach and Tom Rosenstiel, *Blur: How to Know What's True In the Age of Information Overload* (New York: Reprint, Bloomsbury USA, 2011), 126.

2. Paul Krugman, "Reagan Was a Keynesian," *New York Times*, June 7, 2012, http://www.nytimes.com/2012/06/08/opinion/krugman-reagan-was-a-keynesian .html.

3. Michael Dolny, "Think Tank Spectrum Revisited," Fairness & Accuracy in Reporting, June 1, 2012, http://www.fair.org/index.php?page=4549.

4. Steven Greenhouse, "A Campaign to Raise the Minimum Wage," *New York Times*, April 9, 2012, http://www.nytimes.com/2012/04/10/business/ economy/a-campaign-to-raise-the-minimum-wage.html.

5. Michael Cooper, "Many American Workers Are Underemployed and Underpaid," *New York Times*, June 18, 2012, http://www.nytimes.com/2012/06/ 19/us/many-american-workers-are-underemployed-and-underpaid.html.

6. "United States Crude Oil Consumption by Year," index mundi, accessed December 21, 2012, http://www.indexmundi.com/energy.aspx?country =us&product=oil&graph=consumption.

7. "3 to 4.3 Billion Barrels of Technically Recoverable Oil Assessed in North Dakota and Montana's Bakken Formation—25 Times More Than 1995 Estimate," United States Geological Service, April 10, 2008, http://www.usgs.gov/newsroom/article.asp?ID=1911.

8. Jeffrey H. Birnbaum, "Tax Relief in 2000? No Way! Despite Surpluses as Far as the Eye Can See, Partisan Politics and Personal Animosities Will Likely Block Major Tax Relief Next Year," *Fortune*, November 8, 1999, http://money.cnn.com/magazines/fortune/fortune_archive/1999/11/08/268551/index.htm.

9. "Budget and Economic Outlook: Historical Budget Data," Table E-1: Revenues, Outlays, Deficits, Surpluses, and Debt Held by the Public, 1971 to 2010, in Billions of Dollars," Congressional Budget Office, accessed December 21, 2012, http://www.cbo.gov/sites/default/files/cbofiles/ftpdocs/120xx/doc12039/historicaltables[1].pdf.

10. "Our Processes," Congressional Budget Office, accessed December 21, 2012, http://www.cbo.gov/about/our-processes.

11. Edwin Park and Matt Broaddus, "Lower-Than-Expected Medicare Drug Costs Mostly Reflect Lower Enrollment and Slowing of Overall Drug Spending, Not Reliance on Private Plans," Center on Budget and Policy Priorities, May 14, 2012, http://www.cbpp.org/cms/index.cfm?fa=view&id=3775.

12. Brian Faler, "Budget Office Misses on Big Bills Cloud Health Debate (Update1)," Bloomberg, September 24, 2009, http://www.bloomberg.com/apps/news?pid=newsarchive&sid=axAynyxJQILE.

13. " 'Common Sense' Ends the Creek Path Battle," *Faversham Times*, June 15, 2012, http://www.thisiskent.co.uk/Common-sense-ends-Creek-path-battle/story-16376671-detail/story.html.

14. James Lankford, "A Common Sense Solution to the Budget Madness—The Government Shutdown Prevention Act," Fox News, December 6, 2011, http://www.foxnews.com/opinion/2011/12/06/common-sense-solution-to-budget-madness-government-shutdown-prevention-act/.

15. Phil Kerpen, "To Stop the War on American Jobs We Must End Obama's War on Coal," Fox News, September 19, 2012, http://www.foxnews.com/opinion/2012/09/19/to-stop-war-on-american-jobs-must-end-obama-war-on-coal/.

16. Dave Gilson, "109 Things Obama Has Declared War On," *Mother Jones*, February 8, 2012, http://motherjones.com/mixed-media/2012/02/obama-war-xmas-christians-cheerios.

17. Anthony Gregory, "Bush's War on the Bill of Rights," LewRockwell.com, May 14, 2004, http://www.lewrockwell.com/gregory/gregory10.html.

18. "The W Effect: Bush's War on Women," *Democracy Now!*, August 31, 2004, http://www.democracynow.org/2004/8/31/the_w_effect_bushs_war_on.

19. Annalee Newitz, "The Bush Administration's War on Science," Alter-Net, February 27, 2008, 'http://www.alternet.org/story/78056/the_bush_administration's_war_on_science.

# TEN

## Navigating the News

*But to the extent that we too think like savages and babble like idiots, we all share the guilt for the mess in which human society finds itself. To cure these evils, we must first go to work on ourselves.*

—S. I. Hayakawa

### YOU CAN'T CHANGE THE MEDIA, BUT YOU *CAN* CHANGE YOURSELF (MAYBE)

As we've seen, there are an awful lot of incentives for the media to think like savages and babble like idiots. Political news regularly overemphasizes conflict, ignores complexity, encourages our biases, plays on our irrationality, and misuses data—all while trying to convince us that we're getting the whole story. The most common response to this is to blame the media itself, as if the media is part of some massive, fiendish plot to dumb down American political discourse. Maybe there really *is* a massive, fiendish plot by the media to make us stupider, but that seems pretty unlikely. First, massive, fiendish plots are really tough to engineer and even tougher to keep secret (just ask any Bond villain). Second, we don't need to invoke a collusion of evil media barons to understand why we get the political news we get—the news looks the way it does because that's what sells. The only massive, fiendish plot is capitalism, and considering that capitalism is here to stay (which is a very good thing because every alternative to capitalism stinks) we're pretty much stuck with the political news we've got.

Traditionally, the last chapter of a book like this should be all about what can be done to fix the awful problem the author has been going on and on about in the previous chapters. Often, there will be a dramatic call to action urging the implementation of a simple, common-sense plan to fix things. These plans typically involve enormous government intervention, massive societal change, and fundamental alterations to human nature (e.g., "If people would only just really *listen* to each other"). In a (slight) nod to reality, some authors of books like this will admit that their ideas might be the tiniest bit difficult to implement, but that's about it. And readers roll their eyes and think, "Yeah, right. Like *that* will ever happen."

I'm going to stay away from those sort of big-picture suggestions—not so much because they lack merit (though plenty of them do) but because suggestions like that aren't very useful to you in the here and now. Nothing you (or I) can do is likely to change political news for the better; in fact, most of the signs point to increased sensationalism, superficiality, and stupidity in the media's coverage of politics. What you *can* change is how you deal with the political media that's out there. What follows are a few concrete, realistic ideas concerning how you might go about doing that.

## CONTEXT IS CRITICAL

As a fan of good beer, I made a point of visiting a number of English pubs when I had an opportunity to go to London. While the beer was very different from what I was used to in the United States (warmer and a lot tastier, mainly), one thing was the same: sports on TV. Except the sport wasn't baseball or (American) football—it was cricket. I got to London just in time for the first test match of the famed Ashes Series, which pits the United Kingdom's best cricketers against their bitter rivals from Australia. I knew nothing about cricket, but I thought I might as well try to get in the spirit and watch as I drank my pint(s). But no matter how closely I watched (or how many pints I drank) I couldn't figure it out. Wickets fell, batsmen—well, I guess they batted, but it all just seemed like a series of random activities, punctuated by yelling and screaming. My pubmates were alternately superexcited and hugely dejected, but it was all just pointless noise to me.* Before too long, I started to actively dislike cricket, and for the rest of my time in London I tried to avoid pubs that were showing it.

---

*Australia ended up winning by 239 runs, which seems like a lot to me.

The problem wasn't with the game—the problem was with me. I just didn't understand what was going on. Watching more wasn't helping much because the announcers and the fans seemed to be speaking some sort of special language, referring to players, rivalries, and rules that meant nothing to me. Maybe I would have figured it out eventually, but why would I bother to put myself through all the hassle? The broadcast was pretty obviously designed for people who were already fans, not newbies trying to figure out the game. In retrospect, I can understand that; after all, explaining the rules after every play (or whatever it's called in cricket) would be unbelievably tedious to serious fans. But at the time, I wasn't thinking about any of that. I just wanted it to stop.

Politics is a lot like cricket. Both are full of complex rules and long-standing rivalries that take some effort to truly appreciate. Plenty of people don't have a good understanding of the rules or the rivalries, and so they tune out in frustration. Just as it's possible to understand cricket by watching enough matches (or so I'm told) you can pick up your politics solely by watching the news. But in both cases, you're in for a long, rough slog. If you manage to overcome your initial confusion and boredom, you'll probably develop a loyalty to a team (political party) long before you really understand the game because it's a lot easier to root for your side and scream about what crazy things those other people are doing than it is to develop an appreciation for the underlying tactics and strategies.*

The best way to understand the basic rules of politics and gain an appreciation for the historical context that shapes so many current political debates is to take a class or two and read some decent books. If you're currently in a political science class, or you have the opportunity to take one, you're in a good position to get some valuable context. Combine some introductory political science with a modern U.S. history class and you're off to a very solid start. If you're not currently in college, you might want to explore the ever-growing number of free courses available online through services like iTunes U, Coursera, and edX. While free, online courses can't begin to replicate the level of instruction and feedback you'd get from even a mediocre in-person political science or history class, they provide guidance and structure that can be very helpful, especially when you're getting started.

But it's not always possible to find the time to take a class, and even if you can, how much of value you actually end up learning is going to vary a lot—some professors are absolutely amazing, but just like in any other

---

*Tactics and strategies are actually two different things, which lots of people don't realize. Tactics are short-term moves in the service of a strategy, which is a bigger, longer-term goal.

profession, most of us are about average. In that case, you can always do some reading on your own. You won't have the considerable benefit of working with an expert in the field, but self-directed reading is certainly cheaper and easier than any of the alternatives. Of course, if you decide to go this route, you've got to figure out what to read—although there are a ton of political science books out there, most aren't very good. (I've included a number of suggestions in the Appendix to this book, but it's much more of jumping-off point than a definitive list.)

If you do go looking for other books on politics, try to find out something about the author before you start reading. Many of the most popular books on politics are written by people who are a lot more interested in getting you worked up than in putting together good, solid arguments. As a general rule, stay away from anything written by someone on television— that most definitely includes politicians. Autobiographies from people in politics or media can be interesting, but because the author is also the subject, they're a lousy place to go for a reasonably accurate depiction of politics. It's also a good idea to be skeptical of best-sellers, which are usually inflammatory, personality-driven, and largely useless when it comes to understanding anything about how politics works.

The political books most likely to *not* be a waste of your time are those written by social scientists, particularly political scientists, historians, and economists. Unfortunately, a lot of social scientists are truly awful writers, and it can be tough to work through their tortured prose and figure out what they mean. (Or sometimes they're absolutely clear but horrifically boring.) Occasionally, a social scientist will pair up with a print journalist to write, which can help out considerably because it brings together the social scientist's deeper understanding of the topic with the journalist's ability to write in a way that won't bore people to death.

The problem with reading books is that it takes time, and most of us don't have all that much time to spare. If you're currently following political news, you might want to cut back for a while and spend that time with a book. Most political news is largely fluff anyway, and it will still be there after you've read a book or two. When you do come back to following current politics, the more in-depth reading you've done will really help you to better understand how the individual news stories you're seeing fit into the broader context you've acquired for yourself.

This isn't some huge effort—or at least it doesn't have to be. It takes the average reader about 90 seconds to complete a page of nonfiction in a reasonably careful manner. This means that, if you're more or less average, you should be able to finish a 400-page book in about 10 hours. Even if you can only devote 20 minutes a day to that book, you'll have it done in about a month. And after you've carefully read even a few good books on politics, you're going to be much more grounded in the fundamentals than you would be even after years of following the daily political news.

The part about *carefully* reading is important. You can't read a meaningful work of nonfiction in the same way you might breeze through an online article. Rushing is bad, while reading in chunks—ideally, chapter-sized chunks—is good. Even if you don't have the time to read whole chapters at once, try to break up your reading as little as possible and read the book on a regular basis (ideally every day) so you won't forget as much. You should also minimize distractions when you're reading—remember that although you might *feel* like you're multitasking, what you're really doing is rapidly switching back and forth between tasks, making you measurably less efficient at all of them.

Once you've finished a book, you might consider checking out a few reviews so that you can see what others thought about it. This can be an extremely useful thing to do, especially if you're reading on your own. A good reviewer does a lot more than summarize a book—the best reviews will discuss the author, raise issues from the book, suggest counterarguments, and generally point out instances in which the book's author might have missed something. These aren't generally the sort of reviews you'll get from amazon.com (although some amazon reviews can be pretty thought provoking), but all it takes is a few seconds online to find quality reviews of many books on politics. (To help you out with this, the Appendix includes a link to a custom Google search designed to pull up only book reviews.) Just as you should consider the credentials of a book's author, you should also try to find out something about any reviewer—a review coming from a political scientist, for instance, will probably be worth a little bit more than something written by "doodlecat17." Some people like reading the reviews before the book so that they can get a sense of what they're in for. That's a pretty good idea, but you might want to put off looking at any extensive reviews until after you've finished the book, so that you'll go into it without being influenced by the biases of the reviewer.

## BACK TO THE NEWS

The more in-depth knowledge about politics you acquire, whether it's in classes or on your own, the better you'll be able to engage with political news in a truly informed manner. But with so many choices, it can be difficult to figure out a good way to follow the news. The media would really like you to develop a daily (or, better yet, hourly) habit of news-following because it's better for their bottom line. To get you to keep watching and reading, they'll try their best to convince you that every day's news is equally worth your time and attention. We know that can't possibly be true, but knowing it doesn't help much in sorting through the mounds of political reporting and commentary that pile up every minute of every day. Not all that long ago weekly newsmagazines gave people a reasonable way to follow politics on a less-than-daily basis. While some of these magazines still exist, it's been a while since they've bothered trying to provide a coherent summary of the week's events—that would be old news, which in addition to being oxymoronic doesn't interest enough people to be profitable.

Considering the lack of weekly news summaries, there's no good alternative to following the news on a daily, or near daily, basis. If you get your news online, consider using a free service like Readability or Instapaper, which allows you to save online articles and go back to them later. Skimming a few news headlines and saving articles that look potentially important takes only a few minutes a day. When you come back to the news you've compiled at the end of the week, you'll almost certainly find that many of the things that seemed worth reading at the time have faded in importance.

## WHERE TO GO?

By this point, you know that reading is the best way to get your political news. If you have limited time, your best bet is to get your news from a print source, whether it's a physical paper or online. The highest quality, most carefully reported stories generally come from the most prestigious news organizations. In political news the Big Three sources are the *New York Times*, the *Washington Post*, and the *Wall Street Journal*. If you have copious free time, you can look over the political sections of each of them. If that's not possible, consider switching off, reading a different one each day (that's what I do). The basic political news stories they cover are similar enough that you won't miss anything big. The *New York Times* and the *Washington Post* tend to have a bit of a liberal bias (stronger at the *Times* than at the *Post*), whereas the *Wall Street Journal* is a more conservative paper. These biases can be seen mainly in the papers' editorial and opinion sections. If you stick to the news stories, you'll encounter considerably less ideological bias. Checking out these sources on a regular basis doesn't give you balance, exactly, but it's the best way to get a general sense of mainstream thought on both the political right and left. However, with some of the *Journal's* articles available only to subscribers, the *Times* having a limited access model (10 free articles per month), and the *Post* currently considering putting some of its content behind a paywall, this isn't an entirely free option.*

You already know that it's not a good idea to get all of your political news from a single source. If you don't have the time or inclination to visit multiple online sources, a political news aggregator might be your best bet. There are plenty of sites that compile political headlines from a variety of sources, with brief summaries and links to full stories from the sources. As long as you remember that you can't fully understand any political story in two or three lines, news aggregators can be a very useful tool. (A list of some of the better political news aggregators I've come across is included in the Appendix.)

## STORY SORTING

Every day, thousands of political news stories are published, which is great if you're a political junkie but not so good if you don't have hours to spend poring over the latest news. The simplest way to deal with this would be to read only those stories that get top billing. But that isn't such a great plan because, as we've seen, the various biases in *all* media mean that the headline stories aren't always the most important stories. By simply accepting the media's view of what matters most, your view of the political world will be shaped by the biases of the media. Instead of allowing the media to do your news filtering, you can do it yourself by applying a quick sorting method to political news. This is fairly simple because almost all political news items fit into one of four categories, which I've listed below in order of importance:

- *Policy*—Policy articles focus on things that government is considering doing, is currently doing, or has done in the past. Start with these.
- *Politics*—Politics stories are mainly about political strategy, focusing on how something might help or hurt a political party or candidate. Almost all campaign and election stories are politics stories. In the months leading up to elections, political media will be dominated by a special subtype of the politics story called the horse race story, which focuses exclusively on who's ahead of who in the polls.
- *Opinion/editorial*—Most of what's written about politics falls into this category. It's not news; it's someone's view of what the news means

*But considering the low online subscription fees for the *Times* and *Journal* (well under a dollar a day, as of 2012), it's a small investment well worth making if you're truly interested in politics.

and what you should think about it. In most major newspapers you'll find this in a special section for opinions and editorials (often called the op-ed page), though sometimes it's snuck into the real news, labeled "news analysis" (the *New York Times* does this a lot). Opinion stories tend to be the most interesting to read, and, not coincidentally, they're also the most biased source for information about politics. They can often help you to make better sense of the news, but remember to view them skeptically, and always try to learn something about the person writing them.

• *Personality*—These stories are profiles of people involved in politics. These are often lengthy articles in which the author takes you behind the scenes. Often times, these stories follow in the wake of big political events, like the passage of a major piece of legislation, and rely on interviews of multiple insiders who discuss exactly what happened every step of the way. Journalists sometimes call these stories tick-tock pieces because they recount moment-by-moment developments.

Another way to filter is to focus on things that have actually happened, as opposed to stories about what might or should happen in the future. The media love speculation because they can generate an endless supply of it to fill the gaping maw of the news hole. Most political speculation in the media is of very limited value and not really worth bothering with.

## ABOVE ALL, BE CRITICAL

The suggestions I've outlined in this chapter should help put you on the road to successfully navigating the news. Keep in mind, though, that thoughtful consumption of political news isn't something that happens on its own—what we're naturally drawn to is news that excites our emotions, confirms our beliefs, and caters to our irrationalities. It feels good, but in the end it leaves us with an unquestionably warped and incomplete view of the political world. Changing this requires some effort, especially at first. I hope you'll decide to make this effort, and that the ideas and tools we've looked at will make it easier for you to do so. It can be difficult to keep all of this in mind in the real world, and so as a supercondensed summary, you might want to remember these four things:

1. Relax—things are rarely as bad as the media makes them seem.
2. No single story can give you the full picture.
3. Numbers are often misleading.
4. The media is biased. And so are you.

# Appendix

## Political Media Resources

This appendix is full of newspapers, magazines, and online resources that might be useful to you in trying to make sense of what's going on in U.S. politics. This isn't some random grab-bag of things—it only includes books, sites, and tools I've used and can recommend. No sane person could possibly keep up with all these things on a regular basis, and so my suggestion is that you check some of them out and see what works best for you.

There's no TV on this list. As I've said in the book, TV is generally a horrible way to get your political news. If forced, I suppose I'd recommend the nightly news from ABC, CBS, or NBC, but I think they're all bad. And if you're getting your political news from Fox or MSBNC, what you're getting isn't news, it's propaganda dressed up as news. You're better off spending your time watching *CSI* reruns. (At least you might pick up some useful tips about blood splatter patterns.)

This list, with links to everything mentioned, is also available online at navigatingthenews.com. I plan to keep the online list updated and revise it as I come across new things that might be useful. If you have any ideas, I'd love to hear from you: feel free to email me at baranowskim@ nku.edu.

### BOOKS

It's virtually impossible to be politically astute without having read at least a few books. There are all sorts of books on politics, but unfortunately many of the most readable ones are full of bad arguments and shallow thinking, while many of the most well thought out are achingly dull. I've spent a lot of years looking for books that combine good reasoning and careful research with a writing style that won't put you to sleep. Here's what I've got so far:

- *American History: A Very Short Introduction* by Paul Boyer (New York: Oxford University Press, 2012)
  After going on and on about how important in-depth understanding and context is, it may seem strange that my first recommendation is for a book that covers the entirety of U.S. history in 138 pages. But if you're looking for a general sense of the big themes and really important happenings over the course of U.S. history, I don't believe there is anything better than this little book, written by a well-respected historian. I'm hoping that it will whet your appetite and get you to delve more deeply into U.S. history, but even if you don't ever read another U.S. history book, the few hours you spend with this one should make a difference. And like all of the books in the Oxford Very Short Introduction series, it's inexpensive (under $10 online, and even less in electronic format).
- *The U.S. Congress: A Very Short Introduction* by Donald Ritchie (New York: Oxford University Press, 2010)
- *The American Presidency: A Very Short Introduction* by Charles O. Jones (New York: Oxford University Press, 2007)
- *The U.S. Supreme Court: A Very Short Introduction* by Linda Greenhouse (New York: Oxford University Press, 2012)
- *American Political Parties and Elections: A Very Short Introduction* by L. Sandy Maisel (New York: Oxford University Press, 2007)
  If you're looking to brush up on the basics of U.S. politics, it's hard to go wrong with any of the U.S. politics books in Oxford's Very Short Introduction series. They're all written by highly regarded people in their respective fields and are, as the title says, very short. In well under 200 pages (which read even faster because the books are not just short but small enough to fit into your back pocket), you'll get some very useful context about important parts of the U.S. political system.
- *American Dreams: The United States since 1945* by H. W. Brands (New York: Penguin, 2010)
  If you'd like more of an in-depth review of what's been going on in the United States since World War II, you have all sorts of choices. But Brands is one of the best in the business at writing history that real

people actually enjoy reading (as opposed to the history you may have been forced to read in school). You'll get over 60 years in under 400 pages of text, which is a pretty impressive feat of condensing.

- *Restless Giant: The United States from Watergate to Bush vs. Gore* by James T. Patterson (New York: Oxford University Press, 2007)
  This is the most recent volume in the highly respected Oxford History of the United States series of books, written by a historian with a knack for telling a compelling story.

- *A Tolerable Anarchy: Rebels, Reactionaries, and the Making of American Freedom* by Jedediah Purdy (New York: Knopf, 2009)
  Another history book, but of a different sort than those mentioned above. Purdy, a law professor at Duke, has written an intellectual history of the United States, focusing on the concept of freedom—something that has been near and dear to the hearts of Americans since the very beginning. If you're willing to give this book a little time, you might discover that political philosophy can really help you understand U.S. politics.

- *The Broken Branch: How Congress Is Failing America and How to Get It Back on Track* by Thomas Mann and Norman Ornstein (New York: Oxford University Press, 2008)

- *It's Even Worse Than It Looks: How the American Constitutional System Collided with the New Politics of Extremism* by Thomas Mann and Norman Ornstein (New York: Oxford University Press, 2012)
  Political scientists Thomas Mann and Norman Ornstein have been leading authorities on Congress for decades. In addition to their deep knowledge and good writing, what makes their work stand out is their ideological differences: Mann is a longtime fellow of the center-left Brookings Institution, while Ornstein is a resident scholar at the conservative American Enterprise Institute.

- *The Second Civil War: How Extreme Partisanship Has Paralyzed Washington and Polarized America* by Ron Brownstein (New York: Penguin, 2008)
  While politics books from reporters are generally long on anecdote and short on thoughtful analysis, Ron Brownstein's book is an exception. Brownstein, a national political reporter since the early 1980s, has twice been a Pulitzer Prize finalist for his presidential campaign coverage. In 2007, he was honored by the American Political Science Association with a lifetime achievement award in recognition of his contributions to public understanding of politics.

- *The Big Sort: Why the Clustering of Like-Minded America Is Tearing Us Apart* by Bill Bishop (New York: Mariner Books, 2009)
  In *The Big Sort*, the author, journalist, and Pulitzer Prize finalist Bill Bishop draws on the statistical studies of sociologist Robert Cushing to explain how demographic changes have led to a more politically divided United States.

- *Supercapitalism: The Transformation of Business, Democracy, and Everyday Life* by Robert Reich (New York: Vintage, 2008)
  Robert Reich, a secretary of labor in the Clinton administration who is currently a professor of public policy at the University of California—Berkley, examines the changes in the domestic and global economy since World War II and how they have radically altered U.S. politics. One of the best and most readable overviews of how technology and globalization has affected politics in the United States.

- *Winner-Take-All Politics: How Washington Made the Rich Richer—and Turned Its Back on the Middle Class* by Jacob Hacker and Paul Pierson (New York: Simon and Schuster, 2011)
  In this book, political scientists Jacob Hacker and Paul Pierson take a close look at rising income inequality in the United States since the 1980s. They conclude that many commonly cited reasons for increased inequality, such as globalization, technology, and education, don't really explain the growing gap between the haves and the have-nots. They argue that the real culprit is political decisions made by both Republicans and Democrats.

- *Are We Rome?: The Fall of an Empire and the Fate of America* by Cullen Murphy (Boston: Mariner, 2008)
  People are always making comparisons between the United States—the superpower of the twentieth and early twenty-first century—with Rome, the original superpower. Murphy looks at parallels between the modern United States and ancient Rome, focusing on politics as a way of better understanding where we are today and where we might be headed in the future.

## Google Custom Book Review Search

http://bit.ly/RooBbO
People who write interesting political books also tend to be people who have reasonably strong opinions about politics. They're also generally people who can make good arguments for their political positions. However convincing their conclusions may seem, it's always a good idea to try and find out what other experts think about their work. You can always

do a Google search, but you'll have to wade through a lot of results to get to reviews. This custom Google search helps to separate out the reviews from everything else.

## NEWSPAPER SITES

### The New York Times

www.nytimes.com

If you're a conservative, you'll probably hate their op-ed page, but regardless of your political orientation, you should appreciate their political news coverage, which sets the standard for the rest of the media. To get past all the typical newspaper website stuff, try their Article Skimmer (www.nytimes.com/skimmer/) or their iPad app, both of which make going through news coverage even more efficient.

### The Wall Street Journal

online.wsj.com

A lot of the articles are only available to paying customers, but if you're serious about getting a high-quality conservative take on political news, there's no better place to go. Their website is kind of a mess, but they've got a really nice iPad app.

### The Washington Post

www.washingtonpost.com

The only one of the Big Three newspapers that offers unlimited free access (at least as of late 2012—don't expect it to last too much longer). The iPad app isn't nearly as good as what you get from the *New York Times* or the *Wall Street Journal*, but again, it's free.

## POLITICAL NEWS AGGREGATORS AND SUMMARIES

### The Daily Beast's Cheat Sheet

www.thedailybeast.com/cheat-sheet/

I can't recommend the largely superficial and often silly Daily Beast as a general news source, but their Cheat Sheet feature, which briefly summarizes top news topics of the day, isn't a bad place to get a general sense of what's going on. It includes links to the longer articles (from non–Daily Beast sources) on which the summaries are based, so you can go more in-depth if you have the time. It's the first political news I look at each morning.

## National Journal's Need to Know Memo

www.nationaljournal.com/newsletters
Every weekday morning, National Journal puts together short summaries of the top political stories of the day with links to more detailed coverage. I hate e-mail newsletters, but this one packs in so much useful information I don't really mind. (Plus, it's only available via e-mail, so I don't really have a choice.)

## Wonkbook

http://www.washingtonpost.com/blogs/ezra-klein/
Wonkbook is a policy-oriented look at the most important political news of the day. It's part of a much larger site called Wonkblog that will quickly overwhelm all but the most obsessive politics and policy junkies. (The page does have something of a liberal political bias, and I'd love to be able to point you to a conservative counterpart to it. But after years of searching, I haven't found one.) You can have Wonkbook delivered via e-mail every weekday morning by going to the address below. It's free, but you have to fill in a few forms. Don't let that deter you because you won't find a better summary of the nitty gritty of government policy anywhere. (http://www.washingtonpost.com/ac2/wp-dyn/admin/email)

## CNN Political Hot Topics

politicalticker.blogs.cnn.com/category/political-hot-topics/
Longer summaries than you'll find at most aggregators, which is great if you're pressed for time. Unlike its cable news competitors at Fox and MSNBC, CNN actually makes an effort to not be overtly partisan, which is nice.

## MyWay Political News

http://news.myway.com/index/id/politics%7Cap.html
Not a true aggregator because all the stories come from the Associated Press, but its stripped-down format works very well with smartphones and Kindles.

## Real Clear Politics and Real Clear Policy

http://www.realclearpolitics.com/
http://www.realclearpolicy.com/
The best place to go for a wide selection of commentary and analysis on the main politics and policy issues of the moment.

### The Atlantic Wire: Today's Best

http://www.theatlanticwire.com/posts/todays-best/

The top five opinion columns of each weekday, as chosen by the editors of the generally quite-good Atlantic Wire site. (The parent site—theatlantic.com—also has a lot of good political writing and is worth checking out too.)

## POLITICAL BLOGS

### The Monkey Cage

http://themonkeycage.org/

A blog written by some top political scientists, dedicated to providing informed commentary to current political events. A great way to get truly expert, research-based perspective on what's happening in politics. Unlike most political scientists, these guys can write for a non-political-scientist audience.

### FiveThirtyEight

http://fivethirtyeight.blogs.nytimes.com/

Although he's best known for extremely accurate election predictions, Nate Silver blogs on politics between elections too, focusing mainly on analyzing public opinion data.

### The Agenda

http://www.nationalreview.com/agenda

Rush Limbaugh and Glenn Beck have given conservative political commentary a bad name, which is unfortunate because there are some truly excellent conservative political commentators out there. National Review's Reihan Salam, who runs the site's *The Agenda* domestic policy blog, is one of the very best.

### Marginal Revolution

http://marginalrevolution.com/

Tyler Cowen, a moderate libertarian economist at George Mason University, does a fantastic job of explaining economic policy to noneconomists.

### Moneybox

http://www.slate.com/blogs/moneybox.html

Matthew Yglesias's *Moneybox* blog, which looks at current economic policy, is another good economic policy blog. Yglesias, who is more liberal than Cowen, isn't an economist, but he does a good job of intelligently analyzing what's going on in economic policy.

## ONLINE READING RESOURCES

Websites are designed to distract you. To limit the various bells and whistles that are thrown at you, one of the following free services might be useful.

### Instapaper

http://www.instapaper.com/

Instapaper is a tool that allows you to save articles you're interested in reading later. It also lets you to read these articles in a simple text format with minimal distractions. I've found it to be the best distraction-free reading app out there, but there are a bunch of other options for this—most notably Pocket and Readability—that do pretty much the same thing Instapaper does. All of them are available for the main Internet browsers (Internet Explorer, Firefox, and Chrome) as well as most phones and tablets.

### Evernote Clearly

http://evernote.com/clearly/

Allows you to view whatever web page you have in a clean and uncluttered format. If you have an Evernote account you can also use it to save articles for later reading. There are lots of browser add-ons that do this (you might want to try Readable or iReader), but Clearly is the best one I've seen and what I use every day.

## FACT-CHECKING TOOLS

These sites specialize in checking claims made by politicians.

### Politifact

http://www.politifact.com/

A project of the *St. Petersburg Times*, a newspaper owned by the non-profit Poynter Institute for Media Studies. Winner of a Pulitzer Prize for coverage of the 2008 election.

## Factcheck

http://www.factcheck.org/
A nonpartisan project of the University of Pennsylvania's Annenberg Public Policy Center. (No Pulitzer, but really good.)

## Rbutr

http://rbutr.com/
A new approach to fact checking—an app that installs on your browser and searches whatever article your reading for rebuttals. It sounds great in theory, but it hasn't picked up enough users to be really useful yet. I keep coming back to it in the hope it will someday be everything it could be. By the time you read this, Rbutr might be really great or out of business. Worth giving a quick look and trying out for a few days.

## Snopes

http://snopes.com/politics/politics.asp
Snopes checks the veracity of all sorts of stories, particularly some of the crazy things that are sent around the Internet in e-mails.

# Selected Bibliography

Antonakis, John, and Olaf Dalgas. "Predicting Elections: Child's Play!" *Science* 323, no. 5918 (February 27, 2009): 1183.

Burton, Robert. *On Being Certain: Believing You Are Right Even When You're Not*. New York: Reprint. St. Martin's Griffin, 2009.

Carr, Nicholas. *The Shallows: What the Internet Is Doing to Our Brains*. New York: W. W. Norton & Company, 2010.

Cohen, Geoffrey L. "Party over Policy: The Dominating Impact of Group Influence on Political Beliefs." *Journal of Personality and Social Psychology* 85, no. 5 (November 2003): 808–822.

Donsbach, Wolfgang, ed. *The International Encyclopedia of Communication*. 1st ed. Malden, MA: Wiley-Blackwell, 2008.

Downs, Anthony. *An Economic Theory of Democracy*. New York: Addison Wesley, 1997.

Grabe, Maria Elizabeth, Rasha Kamhawi, and Narine Yegiyan. "Informing Citizens: How People with Different Levels of Education Process Television, Newspaper, and Web News." *Journal of Broadcasting & Electronic Media* 53, no. 1 (2009): 90–111.

Groseclose, Tim. *Left Turn: How Liberal Media Bias Distorts the American Mind*. New York: St. Martin's Griffin, 2012.

Jones, Alex. *Losing the News: The Future of the News That Feeds Democracy*. Reprint. New York: Oxford University Press, 2011.

Kahneman, Daniel. *Thinking, Fast and Slow*. 1st ed. New York: Farrar, Straus and Giroux, 2011.

Kosloff, Spee, Jeff Greenberg, Toni Schmader, Mark Dechesne, and David Weise. "Smearing the Opposition: Implicit and Explicit Stigmatization of the 2008 U.S. Presidential Candidates and the Current U.S. President."

*Journal of Experimental Psychology. General* 139, no. 3 (August 2010): 383–398.

Kovach, Bill, and Tom Rosenstiel. *Blur: How to Know What's True in the Age of Information Overload*. New York: Reprint. Bloomsbury USA, 2011.

Lau, Richard R., Lee Sigelman, and Ivy Brown Rovner. "The Effects of Negative Political Campaigns: A Meta-Analytic Reassessment." *Journal of Politics* 69, no. 4 (2007): 1176–1209.

Lawson, Chappell, Gabriel S. Lenz, Andy Baker, and Michael Myers. "Looking Like a Winner: Candidate Appearance and Electoral Success in New Democracies." *World Politics* 62, no. 4 (2010): 561–593.

Manjoo, Farhad. *True Enough: Learning to Live in a Post-Fact Society*. John Wiley & Sons, 2009.

Moore, David W. *The Opinion Makers: An Insider Exposes the Truth behind the Polls*. Hoboken, NJ: Beacon Press, 2009.

Nyhan, B., and J. Reifler. "When Corrections Fail: The Persistence of Political Misperceptions." *Political Behavior* 32, no. 2 (2010): 303–330.

Ophir, Eyal, Clifford Nass, and Anthony D. Wagner. "Cognitive Control in Media Multitaskers." *Proceedings of the National Academy of Sciences of the United States of America* 106, no. 37 (September 15, 2009): 15583–15587.

Pariser, Eli. *The Filter Bubble: What the Internet Is Hiding from You*. New York: Penguin Press, 2011.

Pew Research Center. "The State of the News Media 2012." Accessed December 31, 2012, http://stateofthemedia.org/.

Postman, Neil. *Amusing Ourselves to Death: Public Discourse in the Age of Show Business*. 20th Anniversary ed. New York: Penguin, 2005.

Ramsey, Jennifer L., Judith H. Langlois, Rebecca A. Hoss, Adam J. Rubenstein, and Angela M. Griffin. "Origins of a Stereotype: Categorization of Facial Attractiveness by 6-Month-Old Infants." *Developmental Science* 7, no. 2 (2004): 201–211.

Reid, Scott A. "A Self-Categorization Explanation for the Hostile Media Effect." *Journal of Communication* 62, no. 3 (2012): 381–399.

Schwartz, Barry. *The Paradox of Choice: Why More Is Less*. Harper Perennial, 2005.

Sommerville, C. John. *How the News Makes Us Dumb: The Death of Wisdom in an Information Society*. Downers Grove, IL: IVP Books, 1999.

Szanto, Andras, and Orville Schell. *What Orwell Didn't Know: Propaganda and the New Face of American Politics*. New York: Reprint. PublicAffairs, 2007.

Taber, Charles S., and Milton Lodge. "Motivated Skepticism in the Evaluation of Political Beliefs." *American Journal of Political Science* 50, no. 3 (July 1, 2006): 755–769.

Tavris, Carol, and Elliot Aronson. *Mistakes Were Made (But Not by Me): Why We Justify Foolish Beliefs, Bad Decisions, and Hurtful Acts*. Orlando, FL: Reprint. Mariner Books, 2008.

Tetlock, Philip E. *Expert Political Judgment: How Good Is It? How Can We Know?* Princeton, NJ: Princeton University Press, 2006.

Todorov, Alexander, Anesu N. Mandisodza, Amir Goren, and Crystal C. Hall. "Inferences of Competence from Faces Predict Election Outcomes." *Science* 308, no. 5728 (June 10, 2005): 1623–1626.

Waismel-Manor, Israel, and Yariv Tsfati. "Why Do Better-Looking Members of Congress Receive More Television Coverage?" *Political Communication* 28, no. 4 (2011): 440–463.

West, Richard F, Russell J. Meserve, and Keith E Stanovich. "Cognitive Sophistication Does Not Attenuate the Bias Blind Spot." *Journal of Personality and Social Psychology* (June 4, 2012). http://www.ncbi.nlm.nih.gov/pubmed/22663351.

# Index

## About the Author

**Michael Baranowski** is an associate professor of political science at Northern Kentucky University, where he teaches in the areas of media, American politics, public policy, and research methods. His academic research has been published in *PS: Political Science and Politics*, *The Journal of Political Science Education*, *Simulation & Gaming*, *The International Journal of Public Administration*, *Legislative Studies Quarterly*, *State Politics & Policy Quarterly*, and *Politics & Policy*.